KT-492-823

Building Self-Esteem

SHREWSBURY COLLEGE
RADBROOK LRC

SUE ATKINSON is
the author of *Climbing
out of Depression*, a highly
successful book which
has proved invaluable
to many sufferers because
it is written from the
point of view of a sufferer
rather than an 'expert'.
As well as lecturing in
primary maths education,
Sue works with maths
teachers across Britain
and internationally to
improve their skills. She
has written several books
in this area. She has two
grown-up children and
lives in Norwich.

I want to dedicate this book to two
wonderful women, both of whom I met
in the same year. The first is my precious
daughter Rachel, who burst into my life
one snowy February day. From that first
amazing moment as I held her and looked
at her, some hugely deep part of myself
was changed for ever. The love of that
moment has grown into a relationship
that has profoundly affected our family
and the writing of this book.

The second person is my dear friend, Alice
Petersen. Over the years Alice has been
my friend and 'mother'. Much of this book
I wrote sitting in her house in Pittsburgh
and throughout it are whole sections that
I first thought through because of her
great wisdom and love. In many ways this
is her book. Thank you, Rachel and Alice.

Building Self-Esteem

A Practical Guide to Growing in Confidence

Sue Atkinson

SHREWSBURY COLLEGE
RADBROOK LRC

A LION BOOK

SHREWSBURY COLLEGE LIBRARY

INV. No. L858543   DATE 16/3/04

ORD No. 17559   DATE 4/3/04

ACC. No.   043557

CLASS No.

PRICE 7.99   CHECKED

Copyright © 2001 Sue Atkinson
Illustrations copyright © 2001 Joy Dunn

The author asserts the moral right
to be identified as the author of this work

Published by
Lion Publishing plc
Mayfield House, 256 Banbury Road
Oxford OX2 7DH, England
www.lion-publishing.co.uk
ISBN 0 7459 3113 8

First edition 1993
10 9 8 7 6 5 4 3 2 1

All rights reserved

Acknowledgments
Extracts from the New Jerusalem Bible are published
and copyright © 1985 by Darton, Longman and Todd
Ltd and les Editions du Cerf, and by Doubleday, a division
of Bantam Doubleday Dell Publishing Group, Inc. Used
by permission of Darton, Longman and Todd Ltd, and
Doubleday, a division of Random House, Inc.

Extract from *The Velveteen Rabbit*, © 1992 the Estate
of Margery Williams, published by William Heinemann
Ltd and used with permission of Egmont Children's
Books Ltd, London.

Prayer from *Celtic Prayers* by Robert van der Weyer,
published by Hunt and Thorpe.

Prayer by Reinhold Niebuhr, © the Estate of Reinhold
Niebuhr.

A catalogue record for this book is available
from the British Library

Typeset in 11/13 Baskerville
Printed and bound in Great Britain
by Omnia Books Ltd, Glasgow

Contents

Preface

This book grew out of a life-changing experience I had during some successful therapy to help me through a devastatingly difficult work situation. Out of the difficulties I was facing blossomed feelings about myself I'd never had before.

These feelings were tremendously exciting. They came from deep within me and the transformation was magical. The feelings were that I was a valuable and worthwhile person. Although these feelings did actually only last a few months I went from having been in self-destruct mode for several years to being able to say, very gradually and tentatively, 'I'm OK.'

I began to feel loved, cared for and valued. That love, care and value had been there for years, but I couldn't see it until then. I had persistently stayed in my brainwashed state from childhood, when I was told repeatedly that I was no good, useless, ugly and a terrible person.

I have to admit that I have no idea exactly how or why that change to feeling OK took place, but my main qualification for writing this book is that it did actually happen!

■ The start of the journey

Twenty years ago I had no idea that my fundamental problem with life was that I believed that I was useless and hopeless. I had never heard of 'low self-esteem'.

Then I went to a women's group one evening and the speaker was someone I had known vaguely – our partners were colleagues. She had come to talk as a psychologist about depression which was why I had gone to the meeting that day. She asked us what we thought was the most common problem with which people came to psychologists and psychiatrists. I said caring for young children at home, but she said no, it was low self-esteem. I remember the impact of that moment. Not only had I dared to open my mouth and been seen to be wrong, but I had no idea at all what low self-esteem was. I sat there thinking I could be from another planet for all I understood about what this woman was saying. But she went on to explain that low self-esteem was about having feelings of worthlessness and the way in which some people believe themselves to be no use.

I listened to her and, once I got beyond thinking that she was talking in a foreign language, I realized that she was describing my innermost feelings. How did this woman know that I felt I had no significance? How come she was able to sit there and tell me what I was thinking better than I could have described it myself?

I remember sitting spellbound. Someone had just given me a key to unlock a new part of my life that had been cramping everything that I did and had kept me trapped in depression and anxiety for years. The feelings were huge. There was the thrill of something new, but also the terrible fear of the unknown.

Reading this book might be a bit like that for you. Self-discovery is always at least a bit exciting, but often utterly painful and frightening.

Twenty years later, my work situation fell apart and I ended up in therapy with John.

■ Moving on

Therapy with John was remarkably successful and the beginning of me feeling OK. Then, sadly, I got myself into some pretty disastrous group therapy. By the end of nine months of that, my sense of feeling good about myself had evaporated. I was having panic attacks that were lasting all day. I couldn't even sit and eat a meal with my family. I had so many phobias it was impossible for normal life to go on. I was offered some therapy at a London hospital but that meant sitting in a crowded and smoky waiting room and I just couldn't do that. So I just had to struggle for a few years on my own. That taught me a lot!

Then I started in therapy with Ruth (not her real name). Gradually that magical feeling of being OK began to show that it hadn't completely disappeared. But it wasn't very secure. Most of this book has been written as I work with Ruth and it reflects my attempts to come to terms with my abusive childhood and cope with my complex working life and repeated spells of depression.

■ Starting to write

As I begin to write, I am plagued by terrible self-doubt. I don't have the confidence or the ability to do this. 'How can I possibly do this book?' I asked my family. My daughter looked at me across the table and said with her disarming ability to get to the root of a problem, 'Well, you could always call it, "I can't believe you want *me* to write this book".'

I think I had a naive view that by the time I finished writing the book, I would reach this wonderful position in my life when everything would be sorted and I would be happily and contentedly functioning in the world of family and professional life.

But, of course, life isn't like that. It has taken me more than seven years on and off to write the book. Inevitably it reflects both the 'good' and the 'bad' therapy I have had over the years, my struggles, my hopes, my dreams and my failures.

My insights into what self-esteem is and ways that we can become more able to cope with life are not things I understand as a therapist, psychologist or psychiatrist might. I am writing as a non-professional. My job was a teacher of young children and then later I did some research into my professional role as a teacher, eventually helping students to learn to teach and working with teachers to improve their teaching of maths. But in all of these I found myself concerned with self-esteem.

■ The research for this book

Part of my professional research inquired into how teachers perceive their confidence with teaching maths to young children. I found that the vast majority of teachers were worried about passing on their own fear of maths to the children. Many of them felt that they had been taught maths badly and panicked when they had to do some maths for themselves. I interviewed some of these people in depth and the thing that came through from everyone was a feeling of low self-esteem.

This sense of low self-esteem is very common among British teachers; it is not just about maths teaching. In my work with teachers now, I often find morale very low. Since the mid-1980s there has been one change after another from the government so that teachers feel overwhelmed with administration that distracts them from their work with children, and they are constantly exhausted with the many demands made on them. Yet at the same time teachers are trying to raise self-esteem among their pupils. Their dedication to this is thrilling to see and in the resources section at the back I've listed some books teachers can use for this.

I also contacted depressed people through Depression Alliance and I was inundated with heartbreaking stories of how people thought they had lost their sense of being valuable and worthwhile people.

Some of these stories and perceptions of self-esteem from students, teachers and others have been woven into the text, but of course I have changed details in order to ensure confidentiality. Thank you very much to all those people who trusted me enough to share their journey.

So, my thinking in this book is mainly from things within myself, from therapy with John and with Ruth, from activities I tried, from talking with my wonderful partner, David, from knowing Alice, from issues that arose as I talked to people who also find it hard to believe in themselves and from books I read. Some books were so utterly terrible I want to find every copy and burn them, but some of them were helpful and I've listed these in the Resources section at the end of the book.

Thank you to my loving family, David, Rachel, Jonathan, Liz; and some great colleagues, especially Sharon Harrison; and a big thank you to Maurice Lyon, my editor, who believed in me when I couldn't. You have all become a part of the journey.

A special note for those who are depressed

If you are depressed, go gently with the book. (It is terribly important to go to your doctor if you are depressed.) Some of it is much more robust than you might be able to cope with at the moment. Just leave bits that are tough and move on to bits you can cope with. You'll be able to come back to the tough bits another time.

NOT OPEN
TO THE
PUBLIC

Introduction

> **Bella: The more I think about things, the more I see no rhyme or reason in life. No one knows why some things work out and some things don't; why some of us get lucky, and some of us...**
> **Bernie: Get fired.**

From the film Notting Hill

This book is about a process that a large number of the population are going through – trying to find some personal meaning in the apparent chaos around us and trying to find a way to handle life so that it is less of a disaster.

■ Who this book is for

Many people feel that they are not quite good enough. But some of these people simply do not know that at the root of some of their problems is this very poor view of themselves. They say things such as:

- ■ I'm no good.

- ■ I'm a complete failure.

- ■ I am utterly depressed and can't see it getting any better.

- ■ I don't deserve to be happy.

- ■ I fail at everything I do.

- ■ I wish I hadn't been born.

- ■ My mother always said I was a hopeless person and she was right.

- ■ I would be better off dead.

- ■ I'm a born loser.

- ■ Other people can do things but I just can't; I'm useless.

■ **I'm too ugly for anyone to care about.**

■ **I was hopeless at school because I am really stupid.**

■ **People always reject me.**

■ **I have wasted my life.**

These are all signs of low self-esteem and if any of these ring true for you, this book is for you.

■ How to use this book

This book almost certainly won't have any impact on you if you read straight through it from start to end and then never look at it again! The problem with low self-esteem is that it takes time to work at it so rather than reading this book in the way you would a novel you could:

1. Make it into a rainbow book. You could mark bits of it with a red or other colour of pen the first time of reading, and then come back to it later with different colours.

■ We just don't remember our good intentions, or our ideas and thoughts, or our determination to keep struggling on. If we record them in some way we can have a clearer view of where we have come from and a sense of where we could go.

■ Humans seem to learn by coming back to the same issues at a deeper level. So you aren't failing if you need to keep on working away at something. Life is like that.

■ If, like me, you have to look quite hard for good things about life, making a rainbow book can be a part of your search for rainbows – for the promise of something better to come. Rainbows come after the storm.

■ Sometimes we see rainbows best when the sky is still dark and ominous and we know that there is still much of the storm to get through first. But we know when we see them that at least it is the beginning of the end.

■ **If we make notes in different colours of pen, and maybe date them,
we can see that we have made a bit of progress from last year.**

2. You could start a journal as a sign that you are determined
to do something about your low self-esteem.
3. Just do the bits that appeal to you at the moment and
leave bits that don't seem to hit the spot. You can come back
to them in a few months or years.
4. Do at least some of the activities – they are just that –
activities to grapple with, not just sentences on the page to
read through.

■ **Life is so complex that just reading a book, though it can be a
huge influence, is unlikely to lead us to a place where we can feel
good about ourselves.**

■ **The activities will not all appeal to you, but if you are able to do
some of them, and find at least a little time to write in your journal,
I can promise you some greater personal insights. That is the only
promise though!**

I hope that this book will help you, but I can't promise that
once you have read it you will be OK. In my experience,
growing from our position of low self-esteem to some belief
in ourselves is a very slow and hard process.
But it does happen!

**Low self-esteem manifests itself in many harmful,
unfortunate behaviours and causes untold turmoil
and misery. Studies show that poor school achievement, truancy, crime, violence, alcohol and drug
abuse, teenage pregnancy and suicide, response to
peer pressure, all have strong links to self-esteem.**

Murray White

I hope very much that, as I write about trying to creep out
from behind the brick wall for myself, you will recognize
something of your own struggle.

15

Throughout the book there are 'Positive Pointers' that are things we can think about as a part of our strategies to raise our self-esteem. I'm very grateful to various people who spent time with me brainstorming these. I've added to them from notes in my journal and these strategies are things I've noticed help me to feel better.

Positive Pointers

Make lists of what you need to do each day, then do them. Don't make the lists impossible though! Be realistic. It can help to put onto the list a few things that you've already done, then you can cross them out and let yourself feel good about the fact that you've already made a good start on the day.

If psychologists are to be believed, the single most important fact we need to remember about building up our confidence and self-esteem is that *it is possible to change our views of ourselves* and even our feelings by gradually changing what we tell ourselves. Our negative messages of 'I'll never be able to do that', etc. are to be replaced with 'I can do this. Come on. Have a go.' Amazingly, my experience is that those who say this are right.

Activity

Buy or make a notebook for your journal. Value yourself and your privacy by keeping it in a safe place.

Part I

Life Behind the Brick Wall

I
What Low Self-Esteem Feels Like

I was taught these words by my grandmother as
a phrase that is to be used at *all* times in your life.
When things are spectacularly dreadful; when things
are absolutely appalling; when everything is superb
and wonderful and marvellous and happy – say these
words to yourself: *'This too will pass.'* They will give
you a sense of perspective and help you also to make
the most of what is good and to be stoical about what
is bad.

Claire Rayner

This first section is about what low self-esteem feels like,
what it is and how low self-esteem shows in our lives.

■ 'This too will pass'

For me, over the years I have had an image of myself hiding
behind a solid brick wall. There I am, sitting in this safe
place protected from that terrifying outside world. I'm safe
from people hurting me because they can't get at me. I'm
cut off from things. Detached from the world because it
hurts too much.

I am safe behind my wall but I'm terribly lonely and the
isolation gradually makes its way into me, eventually
becoming unbearable. I have to creep out sometimes, but
then I'm very vulnerable. I've left my protection behind and
I can't cope, so at the first opportunity I rush back behind
my wall.

Talking with many others who have low self-esteem, the
image of the brick wall is one they have too, so I have used
it as a theme throughout the book. Some have told me they

also think of themselves in a dark cupboard, or being lost in a huge ocean, or being overwhelmed by a world of monsters or aliens. Whatever you use for your image, I hope you will be able to relate to my brick wall.

Having low self-esteem is very common. When you listen to some people talking, they clearly demonstrate feelings of inadequacy, believing they are not OK as people. They don't feel at peace within themselves. They feel they will never be acceptable. They feel 'useless', 'worthless' and 'no good'.

■ Feelings

In my research I found the things that people who experience low self-esteem say they feel are very varied. Here are some of the things people said they feel – but you won't necessarily feel all of these:

■ lonely and cut off from others

■ lacking in confidence

■ trapped in your own uselessness – it will never get any better

■ tremendous sadness partly because you feel so worthless

■ incompetent and unable to be a good member of a family, student, parent, partner or do your job well

■ suicidal because if you are such a worthless person you might as well be dead

■ enormous fear about life, sometimes a fear of success or a fear of failure – or both!

■ overwhelming feelings of guilt, and often the guilt is about things you need not feel guilty about

■ overwhelming feelings of shame, feeling inferior to others and that you don't deserve a place on God's earth

■ difficulty knowing what you really feel.

■ How low self-esteem shows itself

People with low self-esteem have usually had the most terrible experiences such as having been bullied at home or at school or abused in some way or have had to face a recent terrible situation such as becoming redundant or going through a separation or divorce from a partner. As an outcome of these events people with low self-esteem may have:

■ difficulty in saying what they want and need

■ a tendency towards depression that does not seem to have an obvious reason (it may not be about some recent event such as being made redundant or the death of someone they love, but it is described as 'endogenous', in other words the doctor is saying it comes from within with no apparent external cause)

■ a sense of insecurity about life – believing disaster is just around the corner

■ eating disorders, either not eating enough, or bingeing and/or overeating and either making themselves throw up or becoming fat

■ panic attacks

■ a tendency to be constantly apologizing and putting themselves down

■ a tendency to underachieve because they don't believe in themselves

■ difficulty making good relationships, maybe ending up in an abusive one

■ difficulty in making decisions

■ an oversensitivity to criticism

■ an oversensitivity to the feelings of those around them, sometimes feeling responsible for others' feelings

■ been (or still be) a part of a dysfunctional family and may now be what Americans call a 'co-dependent' person, meaning they are in

some kind of relationship that isn't very healthy and probably in need of some kind of counselling

■ **difficulty trusting people**

■ **a problem with spending so long looking after others that they neglect to look after themselves adequately**

■ **and so on.**

The key issue here is that we don't feel that we have any value. We think other people might be OK, but we aren't. The reasons for this feeling that we aren't OK vary from person to person, but underlying it all is that something in our past led us to believe that we are no good as human beings.

■ Life is a nightmare

For most of us, any kind of change is very difficult and if you are reading this book for personal development, some kind of change could well take place. Although that is likely to result in long-term benefits, it could well be uncomfortable initially. Facing our feelings of lack of confidence and recognizing deep hurts within ourselves is tough going. It is very much easier to choose not to look at the feelings and to stay firmly shut up behind our wall.

We certainly can't develop overnight. It takes many months and years. Sometimes I shut my feelings down and retreat behind the wall for months at a time. Other times I feel stronger and try to work hard at understanding why I'm so fearful. It's probably a bit like eating chocolate. Sometimes I'm strong and I can get through a day without it. Other days I just can't.

For me, those feelings of having no confidence in myself and being shut behind my wall are a bleak kind of loneliness that makes me feel I must be the only person on the planet who feels so cut off from the rest of the world. When it is really bad it feels that having to go out to work is a nightmare in which I have to walk along the edge of a cliff in a howling gale. The precipice beside me is so close I feel sick. I know I am just about to fall over it to be dashed to pieces on the rocks below. At the slightest thing my heart misses a beat and sometimes the panic attack is so bad I long just to retreat from the whole world and be safe behind my wall where I can sit and feel at least some sense of safety.

■ Life is a drag

Having these kinds of feelings dominating our life is going to drag us down and make just ordinary living so exhausting and demanding that we have little energy left over for doing things we think we might enjoy, if we had the inclination to do them – which often we don't. We start to believe that there is no point in doing anything because life will go on being this bad for ever. We might as well just make our wall into a tower and sit inside it and do nothing.

I sometimes see low self-esteem in very small children that I teach and we need to be aware of this as parents, relatives and teachers. A small boy sits beside me, reading to me. He looks up at me and says, 'I can't read, Miss, I'm thick.' My heart goes out to him. As well as trying to turn him into a confident reader who loves books, I have to boost his self-esteem. I feel rage that at just five years old, he already has this poor view of himself.

The good news is that I have seen children change – sometimes in just a few months. I have heard other people talk of their changes in their view of themselves and I know I have changed. I've touched those magical feelings of being OK a few times. I'd like them to be there most of the time.

Positive Pointers

We need to respect everyone. We might not agree with them. We might even think of them as bad people. But they are human beings and deserve to be treated well and valued as children of God.

Some psychologists say that if you act as if you are the kind of person you want to be, you will become that person!

Wow! That's pretty amazing stuff.

So:

■ **If we act confidently, we will become confident.**

■ **If we act with courage, we will become courageous.**

It's worth a try!

Activity

Try to monitor how much you put yourself down. One way to do this is to look at your use of 'should' and 'ought'. These are words that you might use to put yourself or others down.

'I ought to be able to...' and 'I should have...' can be dangerous ways to start a sentence, so look out for these words in your 'self-talk'.

2
What is Low Self-Esteem?

Clinical diagnoses are important... but they do not help the patient... The crucial thing is the story. For it alone shows the human background and the human suffering.

C. G. Jung

Having low self-esteem is not a kind of disease like having a cold or measles. But it is a bit like having had malaria. It is there within us and pops up to the surface every now and then in an utterly disconcerting way. But it is much worse than something like malaria because:

■ it influences the whole of our life, with unremitting devastation on our day-to-day actions.

■ it affects our thoughts and beliefs about the world.

■ it affects all our relationships.

■ it can mean that we achieve far less than our potential in many aspects of our lives.

■ it lowers the quality of our life.

■ What we believe about ourselves

Self-esteem comes not from a germ, but from our beliefs about ourselves that we developed as we grew up and from the other struggles of life. Presumably this process is very complex with its roots in:

■ the ways that our early families treated us.

■ the culture of the society in which we live.

■ our responses to our wider families, friends (and enemies).

■ our natural aptitudes that we were born with (or without) and our unique personality.

■ Low self-esteem shows itself in surprising ways

For many of us, living with our low self-esteem means that we tend to put ourselves down, or be constantly apologizing. But this isn't the only way that low self-esteem shows itself. Often what people say and what they actually *mean* can be two very different things:

'I'm tough and nothing can hurt me.' (*Really I feel frightened but if I threaten you, I hope you will be so intimidated by me that you will leave me alone.*)

'I know everything.' (*I really feel very insecure and uncertain of myself, but if I keep up this show of confidence and total knowledge of absolutely everything, I hope you won't challenge me.*)

'I'm the life and soul of the party. I'm out every night. I can hold my booze so well you will all admire me. Without me your party will be a flop.' (*If I keep joking and fooling around no one will see that inside I am lonely and frightened.*)

'I'm angry about absolutely everything – the government; the schools I went to; every teacher on the earth; my parents; my boss. Everyone had better keep out of my way, or else.' (*I was so hurt as a child, I can't bear to think about it.*)

'I'm utterly and completely hopeless about absolutely everything in life. I can't even drive. Cooking defeats me. I'm an idiot.' (*No one will expect anything of me if I keep saying I'm useless, so that way I will not fail at anything. I will depend on everyone to do things for me and that way I get a nice cosy life that is completely undemanding.*)

'I could have been anyone I wanted to be had it not been for my incompetent teachers, parents, etc., but because of how they treated me I have to do this menial work. It is all their fault and I resent it and will continue to do so for the rest of my life.' (*Everything that is bad about my life is someone else's fault and there is nothing that I can do about it and it will always be like this. It is far too frightening to think of changing.)*

Positive Pointers

Low self-esteem is all around us. But we can do something about it. We are not stuck in some trap built for us by others.

We are *choosing* to defend ourselves behind our brick wall. (We need that protection because life is difficult. We were hurt. We are confused.)

We can *choose* to try to peep out at life beyond our brick wall, but we realize that life out there is tough. But then, life behind the wall isn't that great either, so we might as well give it a go.

Activity

Think about this statement made by the British scientist Russell Stannard:

You are made of stardust.

There are probably several things that you might think this means. For me it means 'I am special.'

3
Self-Esteem, Selfishness and All That

Women lack self-confidence more than men – it's their besetting sin. My father believed in me – he believed I could do anything and that affected me enormously.

Shirley Williams, British politician

It seems that there are some people who think humans are basically good. God created us and he (or she) said he liked what he had made.

Others think that the bottom line is that we are utterly bad. One book I read about self-esteem holds that, 'Yes, you are utterly "sinful" but don't worry about it too much because God loves you despite you being such a sinner.'

Aaagghhh!

It seems to me that if the most inner part of me is totally sinful, there is really not a lot of point in thinking I can raise my self-esteem. I might as well go on sitting here behind my brick wall, far too ashamed to show my face because of my inner feeling of shame and the knowledge that I am a worthless person.

I think Christians can get their knickers in a twist over some of this – and I include myself in that. But I think Adrian Plass got it right when he said on television, 'God is nice and he likes us.'

We all do things that are wrong and that hurt others and probably get God terribly fed up with us, but he (or she) doesn't stop loving us. Since he made us, he presumably has a vested interest in looking after us come what may – and our apologizing for hurting someone or doing something wrong seems to be a part of the deal. We all are a mixture of good and bad. (We'll keep coming back to this because it is such a crucial aspect of raising our self-esteem.)

So I'll stick with the 'God is nice and he likes me'. By sending Jesus, he went to the greatest lengths anyone could go to tell me that. He didn't have to let himself be nailed to a cross. He could have zapped those high priests and soldiers any time he wanted – thunderbolts being a speciality, I believe.

So if there is something about me that is worth loving, something that is even worth dying for, then I don't need to sit here to hide my shame. I can try to see that if I am loved, then, theoretically I can exist as a free and happy person out there beyond the wall. I matter. I have value.

■ Some of the 'self' words

Some 'self' words are negative and are something to do with our personal ambition, such as when we are willing to tread on others to get ourselves to the top; but others are positive.

■ 'Self-loving' can be an adoring and inappropriate narcissistic love and we might come to a watery end as Narcissus did in the story. But there is an appropriate self-loving we need to develop. We need to care for ourselves, and ultimately to learn to love ourselves unconditionally. (If that hits you between the eyes, don't worry. It used to give me the shakes too. Just lodge it into your mind as something to come back to sometime.)

■ 'Self-centredness' and 'selfishness' are fairly obviously things we want to avoid.

■ I think 'self-worth' means almost the same as self-esteem. We see ourselves as having worth.

■ 'Self-acceptance' means we accept ourselves, just as we are, and it is an aspect of loving ourselves. Whatever we think we may have done that is 'bad' doesn't mean that we are bad people.

■ Then there is 'self-fulfilment'. I think this implies a sense of satisfaction and contentment. I think I felt that when I had children. I felt fulfilled.

But I still didn't have good self-esteem. I'm finding it fulfilling writing this book, but my feelings of self-esteem go up and down. So we can experience self-fulfilment as a separate thing from having good self-esteem.

■ An appropriate understanding of 'self'

We need to take care of our self – our physical body and our inner being. By focusing on our 'self' in an appropriate and caring way, taking time to become a bit more realistic in our thoughts about ourselves, we are not being selfish (though at times we may well become self-centred because that is just likely to happen at times in our struggle), we are trying to get ourselves more balanced. Then we can be a much nicer person to be with!

■ The use of the words 'self-esteem'

I spent a while thinking about all these 'self' words and getting quite confused. Some writers say that 'self-esteem' isn't a very good term so I wanted to think carefully about that.

In the end I decided that I know what I mean by 'self-esteem' and when I tried out the term on some people I knew who also had problems of self-esteem, they all used those words with no difficulty. So I decided that I would use the term 'self-esteem' even though there might be a better word for what I'm talking about.

■ Loving ourselves

Love your neighbour as yourself.
Jesus of Nazareth

I'm still intrigued and confused about loving other people as I love myself. I find it much easier to love other people and I can more easily think about hating myself. I'm quite good at that. But Jesus clearly means that I need to learn to love myself.

That's tough.

Presumably we must get this in balance. If I were to set out to love myself and made that my priority, I think it would go drastically wrong. One of the paradoxes of life that I have learnt is that it is as we nurture and love other people that we become more able to love ourselves.

Focusing on the good

I found that, as I looked back over my teaching career and life as a parent, I felt very good about how much I had worked at building up children's self-esteem. We learn to say, 'Wow! That is just great!' to a small child's efforts at writing a story. It might not be that good, and we point out the things that need improving, but the crucial thing I learnt is that if you focus on the good, things get better. If you put children down, you're in big trouble. They start to believe they can't do it. They lose incentive.

Over and over again, almost everyone I talked to about their low self-esteem said that being put down by teachers, parents and older brothers and sisters, was what they thought was at the root of their low self-esteem.

This paradox of life, that we learn to love ourselves and develop a healthy self-esteem partly by loving others and developing their self-esteem, is an important one, but when I tried it out on a few people, I was fascinated to find that some people think that it is the other way round. They said it is only as we learn to love ourselves that we are able to love others.

Maybe the two processes of learning to love others and love ourselves actually go along together.

Positive Pointers

We will only get over our problems of low self-esteem if we set out to care both for ourselves and for others.

Don't wait for a crisis to find out who your real friends are.

1. Think about loving yourself in the same way that you can love other people. If you are like me it could make you feel a bit uncomfortable and squirmy! I'm trying hard to love myself and I find it can help to do something special for myself.

■ **Have a long slow bath with your rubber duck and killer whale.**

■ **Every now and then spend some time doing exactly what you want to do for yourself.**

■ **Have a treat – fresh raspberries, or stay in bed one morning and read a favourite book.**

2. Can you think of things that help you to feel self-fulfilment? For me these things include writing, sewing patchwork and growing flowers and vegetables.

3. Take a deep breath, read this activity and then ignore it if it is too much at the moment.

Write a list of the things that you like about yourself.

(I find it really hard to do this, but I've been trying to do it in the last few years. When someone first asked me to write this list, I burst into tears! Just in case you feel like that too, I've put this activity here so you can read it, but you don't need to do anything about it yet. Just be aware that we will come back to it in Chapter 32.)

If it is any help, the first thing I eventually put on the list was I like my feet. Well, it was a start!

Part 2

How Did I Get Here?

4

Where Does Low
Self-Esteem Come From?

**If your mother is a worrier and teaches you to worry,
you will become an Olympic champion worrier!**
Dr Desmond Kelly, anxiety and depression expert

This section is about people's stories of where their low self-esteem came from. If we are going to learn to manage our life better, we need to understand more about the many reasons why we retreated behind our wall in the first place.

■ How did I end up feeling like this about myself?

Although some people reported things in their adult life as being the thing they think that led to low self-esteem, by far the majority pointed to something in their childhood.
   Here are some of the things people wrote or told me about:

■ **Being told they were unwanted or feeling unwanted. Often this is reported as being because of a broken family and then acquiring a step-parent and/or step-brothers and sisters. (This doesn't mean that everyone from a split family develops feelings of worthlessness.)**

■ **Some kind of abuse, either physical, emotional, verbal or sexual.**

■ **Being teased – a version of verbal abuse (especially if it is followed by, 'What's the matter? Can't you take a joke?').**

■ **Being bullied at school or at home. (I've already said this, but I was utterly astonished at how common this was and I have tried to make this known to both parents and teachers.)**

■ **Having failures, shortcomings or difficulties emphasized. (For example, one woman who has a physical disability felt she was never really given** a chance. Because she couldn't walk, she found people also thought she couldn't think!)

■ Being manipulated by someone more powerful than themselves.

■ Not being given time by parents, maybe with another child in the family being the favourite, or busy parents, etc.

■ Receiving heavy criticism.

■ Feeling abandoned or rejected. Sometimes this feeling of abandonment was due to a death, or a marriage breakdown, or being split from a brother or sister, or being taken away from one situation and put into another.

■ Feeling the odd one out or that they didn't quite fit into the family. This was true for many people including some who were adopted or fostered, whereas some who were adopted or fostered said this was the one thing that gave them stability and it was their real mother or father who seemed to be rejecting them.

Of course, the reasons why a small child comes to see his or herself as worthless might well be very much more complex than we as adults can remember. It is likely that our feelings of low self-esteem have been influenced by things we may never remember or be aware of. Other people do get some kind of insight into those childhood things once they start thinking about it. This kind of remembering can be sudden and overwhelming, and like a 'flashback', which can be very frightening.

■ We need to feel safe

If you are likely to get this kind of scary feeling when you visit your parent's home, or other frightening places, remember to value yourself enough always to have some way of feeling safe. One of my friends, when she goes to visit her mother whom she finds difficult, always drives so that she can leave at any time if it all gets too much.

Although flashbacks are scary, we can learn from them.

They can help us to see that our low self-esteem isn't our 'fault'. Often it was things done to us as defenceless children. We should have been cared for and protected, but we weren't.

■ It doesn't take much

Some people told me that they really couldn't see why they have such low self-esteem because they had average parents. It seems it doesn't take much to get a child to create that brick wall. Some people couldn't identify much of a reason, though mild teasing and parents having very low expectations feature for several people. (Maybe there isn't such a thing as 'mild' teasing?)

Others just talk of one or two incidents which they say were insignificant things. When these are talked about they sometimes show they clearly weren't 'insignificant'! It is very common for people to 'forget' the bad things about their childhood or to play them down.

■ Low expectations

I have taught some children who by a very early age form the belief they are no good. Sometimes I observed things that looked very minor and were said and done by parents of my class whom I considered 'good' parents. On more than one occasion, I found parents saying to me things like this: 'Well, I was no good at maths so I don't suppose he will be either'. Her six-year-old child was standing beside her. All my work to try to get this child motivated and feeling that he could do his work was probably lost in those few seconds! Usually this mother was caring and loving, but this example brings up the whole issue of the influence of low expectation.

If the culture of low expectation were to change, under the same budget we could achieve a 30 per cent increase in educational achievement.

Tony Blair

■ Childhood interpretations of life are complex

To a child, some things that look minor to us now as adults can influence the whole of the rest of their life. Looking back, if adults see that they might have got something out of proportion is in itself a reason to feel bad about themselves.

> My mum died when I was six and I think I went into my shell. Now I'm too shy to go out, but I don't want to spend all my life on my own. But I don't feel brave enough to get out there and meet someone.
>
> Diana, age 29

> Dad left us when I was 11. I thought it was my fault and I was so unhappy. My school work got worse and worse. Now I have this menial job but I know I could have done better. Mum tells me to go to college but I don't think I could.
>
> Alex, age 26

> My mum was fat and I was ashamed of her. Then I put on weight too and I was teased. 'Fatty', they kept saying. I think I must have eaten for comfort and now I don't know if I can stop. I feel so ugly and I hate my body.
>
> Alison, age 24

> I had asthma as a child and I couldn't do things others could do. I knew I was odd, different. I thought I was such a useless person. I realize now that I shouldn't have felt that, but I did. I feel pretty stupid.
>
> Derek, age 31

Each term one in four primary school children report being bullied, and one in ten secondary school children. Some dozen every year suffer so severely they kill themselves.

Many others attempt it in a cry for help. Most say

they dare not tell anyone for fear and for shame at their own feeble inability to stand up for themselves.

Polly Toynbee, British journalist

■ Low self-esteem as an adult

It isn't just in childhood that we can come to see ourselves as worthless. Things happen to us in adult life that can influence the ways in which we see ourselves. The kinds of things I mean are:

■ Being unemployed (long-term unemployment for a young adult who has not had a job since leaving school must be particularly painful).

■ Being made redundant.

■ Any kind of rejection from an individual (such as a relationship breaking down) or from some organization or system (such as perceiving a hospital or school as not caring about us). Trying to get some kind of justice from a 'system' where no one is apparently responsible is so hard that many of us give up and then harbour the resentment of that rejection.

■ Any kind of failure such as not getting the job because we perceive ourselves as failing to do the interview well, or not getting shortlisted in the first place, or anything where we think that it was our 'fault' that something didn't work or happen because we were less able than we thought we were.

The failures and rejections don't need to be the obvious kind of dramatic life event such as a divorce. They can be the seemingly little things such as perceiving ourselves as less worthy because of putting on a bit of weight, or going bald, or growing older.

It is not the scale of the event, but our interpretation of it and what it means to us in our inner world that influences us, so that we conclude we are unworthy or unacceptable.

I suppose I don't expect anything different. I feel that I deserve my life to be like this.

Pam, age 26, whose marriage has just broken up

■ Life events

Some people develop low self-esteem after a big life event such as their house being burgled, a serious illness, the loss of a job, or the loss of someone they love. A young man on a television show about victims of violence described how he lost his self-esteem after a man shot him and other people on an underground train. He said:

> **[The mugger] took my manhood away. He wrecked my self-esteem. I felt so helpless... But now I have built myself up... got my self-esteem back again. It has been hard work, but I did it and now I feel good.**

■ The link between depression and self-esteem

> **When my mum died my dad seemed to go in on himself. He sits all day and just stares out of the window. He got the sack from [his job] and that destroyed him. He just says it is all hopeless. He is hopeless at everything. Now he doesn't even go down the pub. He lost all confidence in himself. He's not so down now, but he still doesn't believe he can do things. He says there is no point trying. The tablets helped a lot, and now me and my sister do all we can to get his confidence back. It is like he feels that he can't do anything properly so he doesn't try.**

Shelly, age 23

Many of the people I talked to were depressed like Shelly's dad. There is a close link between depression and low self-esteem. Sometimes it isn't possible to say what came first, the

39

depression or the low self-esteem, but it looks to me as if both things influence the other and they pull you down. It is this spiralling down into the chaos of it all that often needs some kind of medical help, so if this sounds like your problem, go and see your doctor. Anti-depressants are not addictive and can transform your life.

■ What happened in maths lessons?

From some case studies I did about people's fear and loss of confidence with maths, the dominant thing was being told that they were no good and failing at maths at school. Here are some of the things people wrote about and said:

> We had these multiplication tables tests every Friday after morning assembly. The teacher made us all stand up and then he would fire questions at us and if we could answer quickly we could sit down and we were asked no more questions. If we couldn't answer in time we had to stand on our chairs. Then he would come back to us and if we still couldn't give a correct answer in the time we had to stand on our desk. You could only get to sit down by answering a question quickly, but I never could. I was always the one left standing on their desk at the end and everyone used to laugh at me. I was only seven then and I knew I was no good.
>
> Cassie, a mother with three children
> all now experiencing similar fear with maths

> All through junior school I was always hopeless at maths. Then in secondary school it got so bad that I had to have special tutoring. That worked quite well for me and eventually I got my GCSE maths on the fifth attempt so I could get into college... I'm dreading teaching it but I chose to teach [young children up to age eight] because the maths wouldn't get too hard. You will need to

explain lots of things to me because I won't understand.

Grace, a student teacher, age 42

I'm just hopeless at maths. I always have been. I just can't do it. I don't have that kind of mind. I'm more creative and poetic and maths never interested me... We had a teacher at school when I was six and she said I was hopeless at maths and I suppose I just believed her.

Emma, a student teacher, age 22

Embedded in these stories there is a clear sense of being unable to do things, of forming an opinion about personal capabilities from a very early age. For many of the students I taught at college there was a blank refusal to believe that anything could be done about the situation.

■ Losing belief in ourselves

The very first class I ever took as a teacher was a class of 14-year-olds for maths. I wasn't yet a qualified teacher but in those days you could work as a teacher as soon as you graduated, so I was earning money by standing in for a teacher who was ill. I was given some incredibly tatty and dull maths textbooks and told which page to teach.

The children sat and stared at me as I told them what I had been told to ask them to do. The set page was boring and totally incomprehensible to both me and them, so I suggested we could talk about computers and what they can do and what use computers could have in the future. A few chirped up at this idea and something resembling a discussion started. Then one of the very large sullen boys in the back row said, 'You can't teach us anything, Miss, we're 4E. We're dim.' (In this school all the bright children were put in the A classes, then the B, C, D and finally E.)

He was pronouncing himself unteachable. He had given up. After what might have been just a fifth of his lifetime he was categorizing himself as beyond help.

I felt devastated. That statement had a profound effect on me then and throughout my teaching career. Many of my underlying beliefs about education have developed in the ways they have because of the words that young man spoke. I so much hope that those young people have gone on to find value and love.

■ Giving up

It is this sort of giving up that can become an unhealthy part of our low self-esteem. As one person put it to me: 'Sue, I honestly cannot see that it will ever change. Life has passed me by.'

We must not give up, because things *can* change.

■ **I have seen children change.**

■ **I have seen student teachers change from a quivering mass of tears and migraine headaches at their first maths education workshop, to successful qualified teachers doing maths as their special study.**

■ **I have watched adults get better from depression and have watched their self-esteem blossom.**

■ **I have seen myself change.**

Positive Pointers

It is fine to feel like a helpless and abandoned little child sometimes. To feel like that is OK. I used to think it really silly, but I'm discovering that if we think about that hurt little child within us, it can be a healing part of our struggle to understand ourselves more fully. So talk to that frightened inner child. Reassure him or her that you are going to listen and comfort them. This isn't loopy stuff! It really can help and there is more about this later in the book.

1. Jot down some of the things that you think have contributed to your feelings of low self-esteem. Do it quickly and don't think too much. Often our first reactions will be reaching 'deep' bits of ourselves. And definitely don't judge yourself – 'I'd better not write that down, it isn't very nice.'

Go for it! No one else is going to see it and maybe expressing a fair bit of anger will be the thing that makes the first chink in your brick wall.

2. Start to think about your 'inner child'. If this is a new idea to you, just make a few notes in your journal about what it might mean for you.

5
What is Happening?

It struck Simon for the first time in his life that he was totally unique. In the whole history of the universe, there had never been one of him before. There would never be another.

Anne Fine, *Flour Babies*

A few years ago, when I was having some very successful therapy with John, he started trying to tell me that every baby arrives into the world with value. He had listened to me state quite clearly that it was my fault that my mother's life was so hard, that my family broke up, that others in my family were so disturbed, that my life was so difficult, etc. I said that it was all my fault because I was born.

I remember that moment as he said, 'Sue, it is very hard to think how anyone could blame the *baby*.' My mind went into chaos. As I thought about that moment over the next few months I found that almost all of my view of myself was based on my belief that 'it' (by which I seemed to mean, the chaos of my birth family and the unhappiness of my mother – a thing I was taught was the most important thing in the universe) was *all my fault*.

Gradually I came to see that my basic belief was wrong. How could anyone possibly blame the baby? I didn't ask to be conceived. If my mother had not wanted a baby she should not have had sex with so many men, should she? I began to see that she needed to take some responsibility for the choices she had made.

■ Are we thinking logically?

If we were abused as a child, we were the victim. It was the adults in the situation who had all the power. They were in a position to care, but often they did not. Things were done to us. We were the 'victim'. It was not our fault. (I do wish I could really believe this for more than about two seconds at a time.)

I was learning in therapy that the things that we hold onto deep down inside our inner selves are not always things that are about logic. They are things that are about feelings, about things we learnt when we were tiny, often when we did not have words to explain things to ourselves or others. We are also capable of holding to beliefs that are in conflict with each other. So these things within us need to be unpacked not just with words and with our minds, but with some kind of engaging with our inner person, our spirit, our soul.

This seems to be a very mysterious process and is presumably what you need to learn about to be a psychotherapist.

In my nine months of 'bad' therapy, a few years after ending with John, the new therapist would keep saying to me, 'Oh, Sue, you keep trying to rationalize everything. You intellectualize all the time.' I did not know what to make of this except that I was in some way doing it wrong. Presumably I was 'thinking', not 'feeling', and she didn't like that. But what I had worked at with John had eventually satisfied me intellectually. I found some logic within the whole tangled mess. So it seems as if making sense of our lives is not just about 'feeling' whatever that deep inner tangle is, but also about making sense of it.

■ What are the beliefs we live by?

We all have some kind of beliefs or code of life that we live by. Some people call this their 'religion' or 'philosophy of life' and even people who insist they do not have this 'religion' or 'philosophy' do really, because to say that you live by no set of beliefs is to have a set of beliefs.

I had a set of beliefs about teaching children, starting with the belief that all I did as a teacher was based on respect and value for every child.

Then it hit me – I was not thinking about that value for myself!

I began to see that I was being completely illogical and that shook me rigid.

■ We can be brainwashed

Knowing we need to change our fundamental beliefs is scary. I was believing what my birth family told me, that everything bad was my fault. Yet as an adult I was holding the view that every child is to be respected and valued. These two beliefs were in direct conflict with each other and it took many months to reconcile these beliefs – actually I am still working on it. I am coming to see I had value, too, when I was born. I was just brainwashed into believing I did not.

I can see that it is sometimes a lot more comfortable for me to find reasons to continue to sit here behind my brick wall where I feel safe.

■ Old tapes

Lots of what we feel, do, think and say is not about logic. Our feelings and beliefs seem to be all mixed up and entangled with what we have been told as children and the inner messages that we give ourselves, many of which are completely unconscious.

One of the most helpful things that anyone ever taught me, I learned from my dear friend Alice years ago. Alice said that we have these 'old tapes' playing in our head that are to do with 'stuff' from the past. I have this mental image of an old and battered tape recorder playing me all the old 'stuff' from my childhood home – 'You're absolutely hopeless' and all that. It goes on, and on, and on.

I think we all probably have these negative 'old tapes'. The difference between me and a more 'together' person might well be that they have more positive 'old tapes' and keep their negative 'old tapes' in better control than I do. Maybe they have even learnt to switch their negative stuff off.

The thing we need to grasp here is that if we are listening to these 'old tapes', they are going to keep us feeling bad about ourselves because we are believing all those lies. If I am actually telling myself I am hopeless, I am not letting myself feel and acknowledge my value as a person.

■ Every baby has value

Babies arrive with huge value. The value of a person is not something that comes to us along the way. It is about our existence, not about something we earn.

We are born valuable. We are uniquely special, every one of us. You can see that in the way the doctors and nurses treat the newborn baby. The doctors and midwives take hold of the little person with care, they smile, they assess quickly what must be done to ensure life. Is she breathing? Is she responding? Is an incubator needed?

Then they wrap her and give her to you. This new little person is fresh from God and of inestimable value. This giving of value to the newborn is just the way the world works. We have this instinctive drive to protect our young. It is about the survival of our species, but also goes well beyond that. Most people are horrified at the thought of someone hurting a child. Those who abuse children are reviled. This is evidence that within humans there is this recognition that every child has huge value and significance.

Babies do not come into the world believing that there is something wrong with them. They arrive pleased and curious and ready to complain when something is not to their liking. But soon it is made clear to them that their complaints are not acceptable. Babies find this unfair, and then it is made clear to them that they themselves are not acceptable.

Dorothy Rowe, *The Successful Self*, p. 156

To have the world full of happiness, peace, love and justice, humans need to be given value by those around them. That is what makes society operate well. If relationships, families and basic structures of society, such as laws about caring for others, falter and disintegrate, it is because of some wrong-doing in society.

For me, my value is also there because I believe that God values me – and every other human being. You do not need to believe in God, though, to believe you have value. If humans were to operate as if people were not valuable, the world would be even more full of greed, wars, abuse and injustice than it already is.

■ Many children are not valued

So, I am saying that all humans have value. However, not all humans are given value by those around them. Not giving a baby value results often in low self-esteem, crime, sadness, violence, deep unhappiness, depression, suicide and all the other features of a life not given the respect and worth it deserves. Those who abuse children were often abused themselves, so the loss of value goes on down the generations.

It is something within the adults that can mean that the baby isn't valued. But whether she is put down the sluice, abandoned, given away, has a disability or is loved with all-consuming passion, her value remains the same. She *is* valuable despite the circumstances.

> **Whoever humbles himself like this child, he is the greatest in the kingdom of heaven. Whoever receives one such child in my name receives me; but whoever causes one of these little ones who believe in me to sin, it would be better for him to have a great millstone around his neck and to be drowned in the depth of the sea.**
>
> Jesus of Nazareth

Positive Pointers

Trust your inner self.

We absolutely must not compare ourselves with others (unless we are using someone we admire as a role model and working at being more like them). If we catch ourselves at unhelpful comparing ('He's a much better person than me') where we put ourselves down, we must be firm with ourselves. It has to go.

Everyone that Princess Diana touched went away feeling they were special.

Chris de Burgh

Activity

1. If you feel you were hurt as a child and not given value, try writing about it. Start with: 'I remember when...'. It is OK if you end up angry, in tears of rage, or depressed. To be hurt as a child is an utterly terrible thing. We can start to help ourselves to recover from it when we realize it was world-shattering for us. If we are prepared to say, 'Wow, that was absolutely terrible', then we have some chance to start to put our lives back together again.

2. Think a little more about your hurt inner child.

6
Trying to Live Up to Expectations

**Doing drugs and having unsafe sex is a slow suicide.
It is about people having low self-esteem and feeling
bad about themselves.**

An American psychologist on the BBC

I was feeling ecstatic. I walked out of the shop feeling that
life was OK after all. I had managed to get into a pair of size-
10 trousers and I knew I was now going around with an
idiotic and smug grin on my face.

I knew the truth was that the trousers were very generously
cut and with an elasticated waistband. It wasn't really that I
had suddenly shrunk two sizes but that this year's style was
distinctly baggy and so the trousers accommodated and
disguised my ever-increasing bulges.

Western culture seems to be blaring out messages that we
need to look like the models who strut along the fashion cat-
walk and star in the big films. The fact that they all look as
if they live on fresh air and those gucky meal replacement
drinks just passes us by and we look at them and think, 'I
need to look like that'. We have to look like the perfect
hunky man in the right brand of jeans, the perfect woman
that our culture has developed for us to strive for.

■ We pick up messages from the culture around us

The adverts on the television tell us that we must drive the
right kind of car, drink the right kind of coffee, dress in
'cool' clothes, buy a mobile phone, listen to the latest music,
have model children that go around in dazzlingly white
shirts, and spread the right kind of margarine on our bread.
The right product promises a healthy heart, days of endless

sunshine, adoration from all the people we want to impress and a free plastic boomerang if we send in a thousand special tokens by the end of next week.

■ Expectations of those around us

We are all probably influenced by other people's expectations. The young teenage girl picks up the message without knowing it that to have a figure anything less than one on 'Baywatch' is not all that acceptable. So she learns to hate her body. She goes on crash diets, starves herself, all in the belief that this will make her more acceptable.

> **I was a bit overweight as a child and I was teased. So I began to withdraw. I ate for comfort. I knew I was fat and ugly. Every time I stopped eating I lost weight, but as soon as I started eating again I ended up even bigger. By the age of 23, I was 22 stone and I never went out of the house I was so ashamed.**
>
> Barbara, age 34

The expectations can come from our friends, the newspapers and magazines we read, the advertisement hoardings we see on the way to work and on television. And these adverts use our susceptibility. We are promised a perfect figure if we just use this product, flawless skin if we use that, a sun tan to die for if we use their lamp, this particular brand of fake sun tan cream, and so on.

■ Conforming to the media message?

The adverts seem to encourage us to aim to be perfect. Ageless. Always smartly dressed in the right colour for this year.

These cultural expectations we could observe and comment on as being unnecessary pressures that we all have to live with except for one crucial thing – almost all of us collude with what the media push at us!

(I found it very refreshing that some of the people who read a draft of this chapter said that they did not feel any pressure at all from the media! That is very impressive – and encouraging!)

■ Expectations of being perfect

Perfection is not just about how we look. Some of the people I have talked to about their low self-esteem tell me they came from families where to be anything other than perfect was not tolerated. Sometimes this was about behaviour or looks, but most often it was about achievement at school.

Julie told me of how her father looked at her school report in which she had grade 'A' for everything except for maths for which she had 'A minus'. He glared at her and asked her what on earth had happened to maths? If she could get 'A' for everything else, she should have got it in maths too. He made no comment about all the 'A's other than that. She knew that whatever she did, she was not coming up to his standard. Julie took to compulsive eating and by the age of 18, she was 15 stone.

■ Our reactions to unrealistic expectations

This kind of story about unreasonably high expectations was told to me over and over again by people of all ages and all kinds of backgrounds and current employment and living situations. Some of these people were still full of enormous and rather frightening rage.

My father and mother were quite sure of what they wanted of me. I was to get to university. Both of them had gone to university, but not to Oxford or Cambridge. From the earliest that I can remember I was told that I was to get to one of those. It wasn't going to be good enough to go anywhere else. It hung over me all my school life. If I wasn't getting top marks in a test I knew I wasn't going to make it.

I knew I couldn't do it. I wondered if they would still want me near them if I failed.

Minal, age 20

My father was totally clear about what he wanted. I was to be a champion swimmer. From the age of four he took me swimming and by the age of six I was doing lengths of the baths four times a week before school. Nothing else seemed to matter except my swimming. Even on holiday we had to go where there was a pool so I could train. Of course, by the time I was eight and nine I was pretty good, but that wasn't enough. I had to be the best, and if I was beaten in a gala he would blame me and make me train more the next week. It wasn't good enough to be good. I had to be the best.

Tony, age 32, who had suffered from depression since the age of 17. He had got into university but dropped out owing to his depression.

■ Being the best

Unnecessary competition is something I have watched in schools and wondered just how helpful it is. I think it is important to get a balance.

■ Children love racing to be first to get to the park – but if they race with a sibling, the younger child feels they can never win.

■ Children love to play a match against another school, but team fervour can get horribly out of control.

As a teacher I tried to focus on what each child was good at so that those who hated games could be praised for their brilliant model of a windmill, and those whose models were a total mess were praised because they could hold the whole class together with a regular beat on the drums.

As a mother I used some rewards, but I didn't want my

children to do things just for the reward. But it felt good to be able to say how well something was done and to be able to have a treat.

It is when people think they have to be best that the trouble comes: the young businessman who wants to get to the top however little he sees his family; the young music student who wants to be a concert pianist whatever the cost.

The problem with this kind of experience of having to be best is that it teaches us a very dangerous message – that to be valued we have to achieve. But our value is independent of what we achieve. Schools are often very bad at communicating this message. The child who goes to university is no more or less valuable than the child who leaves school with no qualifications.

■ Being 'good enough'

One of the things people told me about my book, *Climbing Out of Depression*, is how much it has helped them to think about just being 'good enough', an idea originally put forward by Donald Winnicot.

We do not need to be a perfect daughter, a perfect parent, a perfect lover, a perfect taxi-driver or accountant or clown or bricklayer or waiter or student. We just need to be 'good enough'.

Positive Pointer

We do not need to live up to what anyone expects of us. We just need to be ourselves – and that is good enough.

Activity

Think about things that you try to do too well. Write some sentences like this:

54

■ I could try to be just a 'good enough' mother/child/doctor etc.

■ I could try to be just a 'good enough' friend to… and maker of beds, taxi service to school, etc.

If you are like me, you will need to come back to the whole idea of 'good enough' over and over again. It is all too easy to get into the 'I must be perfect at everything' trap.

Part 3

Trapped Behind the Wall

7
Shame and Guilt

Becoming depressed may be the sane person's way of coping with all the madness in the world.

Janet Daley

This section is about those thoughts and feelings we have that are trapping us behind the brick wall.

Quite a lot of our feelings of low self-esteem seem to be about a sense of shame and feelings of guilt, and it is often these feelings that can pull us down into depression.

■ **We remember with shame things we have done. This is the source of our guilt.**

■ **We remember with shame the things that we were told about ourselves as we were put down needlessly.**

■ **We remember a wrong or embarrassing thing that we did, then we tell ourselves that because of that wrong thing, we are for ever condemned. We brand ourselves for ever as liars, thieves, idiots or whatever.**

It is as if we are saying to ourselves, 'I did this unwise thing and now I'm totally evil.' This is an outright lie!

We have translated a feeling of unworthiness about ourselves for what we did into a deep shame about who we are. It is absolutely crucial that we grasp we have made a very unhealthy shift from what we did, to telling ourselves that we are therefore unworthy people.

The feelings of shame are about our very *selves* – not about some bad thing we *did* or *said* but about who

we *are*. It tells us that we *are* unworthy. Totally.

Lewis Smedes in his helpful little book,
Shame and Grace (his emphasis)

■ So we feel unacceptable and unworthy and that we will never be any good.

■ We despise ourselves, and the shame that we feel is the root of our feelings of low self-esteem.

■ Because we feel this shame we want to build ourselves a good strong wall to hide behind and maybe even make it into a tower so that no one can see us and at last we will feel safe and we cannot pollute anyone in the world out there.

■ We feel inappropriate things

When we feel this guilt and shame of low self-esteem, we need to remember that many of the emotions we feel and the characteristics that we give ourselves ('You are such a loser', and so on) are wrong and inappropriate.

To feel

■ 'useless'

■ 'a waste of space'

■ 'ashamed of being such a feeble person'

or whatever your put-you-downs are, is 'stuff' that is misplaced. (Here's me sounding as if I don't do it!)

We all have this 'stuff'. I don't quite know what else to call it. It is the junk we have picked up over the years from those who put us down.

■ Guilt

If we have actually done some wrong, maybe hurt someone deliberately, or lied, or whatever, then the guilt we feel is healthy and it prompts us to say sorry. If we are truly sorry then the guilt will probably go away. In an ideal world presumably it would automatically go alongside the penitence, but if you are like me, you probably let the guilt hang around your neck as you sit behind your wall.

I find I struggle with feelings of hate and then feel guilty, but one of the things that I am learning in therapy is that hate is actually OK. I think somewhere along the line I picked up the view that hate is a terrible thing to feel. But I feel it anyway, so I am just beating myself up if I cling onto guilt for feeling that hate. It would be better to put my thoughts and energies into something positive, such as reassuring myself that I need not turn that emotion of hate into any hateful act.

■ False guilt

When I was talking with people as I wrote this book, I was relieved to find that many people are just like me and feel guilt for things that they are not actually responsible for. This is false guilt. One example of this was a lovely young woman who told me that she feels enormous guilt because she cannot bring herself to go home. Her father sexually abuses her and her mother knows about it. And this lovely young woman is the one who feels the guilt!

■ Our worst things

I asked people if they had particular things that were their 'worst things' – things that really got to them and sent them to rock bottom. Here are some of the things that people identified:

■ being with their parents

■ seeing someone who reminds them of their mother/overcritical father/teacher

■ feeling put down

60

- having to say something publicly

- going to the doctor

- needing to make a very difficult decision

- being in a situation of conflict

- being criticized.

I was very relieved about the last two. Those are things that really get to me. They are my 'worst things'.

I try desperately hard to get better at handling conflict and criticism, and I can see that I am improving, but I can still feel so crushed by it. Presumably this is because I don't yet have enough personal strength and self-esteem to respond appropriately, listen to what is being said and then either accept it or explain why I did something in a particular way.

I asked people what they did when they felt crushed and defeated, and they just wanted to get behind their brick wall. Again, there were a number of different responses:

- eat something (Yes! Chocolate to the rescue.)

- drink alcohol

- cry

- rip up phone books

- go into a rage

- play very loud music or sit and watch television

- hide away from everyone.

The things I do (as well as eat chocolate and cry) are to find my teddy bear and retreat somewhere safe such as my bedroom where I can see my pictures of penguins and puffins and I can look at my special things that hold good memories for me.

Positive Pointers

Every year set yourself an achievable target.

Spend time with people who inspire you and who make you laugh, not with those who irritate or bore you.

Stop for just a moment as you get out of bed, and do a run through of your day in your mind, putting a really up-beat tone to everything. For example, I have been trying to visualize myself eating a sensible breakfast, dealing efficiently with my post, then settling down to writing with a smile on my face. (Surprisingly, smiling really can make us feel better.)

Decide on some alternative drinks to caffeine-laden coffee. Herbal teas can be more relaxing, help you feel better, and are better for reducing stress.

Activity

1. Feeling ashamed of who we are is totally inappropriate. Write in your journal about your feelings of shame so that you can clarify what you are thinking.

2. In your journal describe the kind of person you would like to be: loving, kind, generous, honourable, grateful, compassionate, discerning and so on. Instead of thinking that you just could never be like that, try to be more positive and work towards being that kind of person. Start small. You could decide to do one kind thing every day for a week just to get you going.

3. False guilt is 'stuff' to dump. Look out for those guilty feelings. If you have done wrong, try to put things right, but if it is false guilt, become more aware of it and try to let it go. (Easier said than done, I know!)

4. Identify your 'worst thing'. Try writing in your journal over the next few weeks about why this thing is so big for you. It can help if we know why something affects us so deeply.

5. Plan a strategy for what to do when your 'worst thing' happens. If we can plan ahead for how to handle those really terrible moments, we are well on the way to deciding to defeat our feelings of low self-esteem.

8
Learning to Deal with Anger

**The use of body, mind, emotions and spirit as a totality
is the constant challenge for all of us.**

Jack Dominian, *The Capacity to Love*

I feel a seething rage inside me. One of my team members
at work has let me down again and again. She tries to
control me – a bad idea for anyone to try to do! If I try to
discuss her work with her in an adult way, she flies at me and
shouts and self-justifies, so I back off and tell her that
everything is OK – even though it isn't. Anything, including
lying, comes into play as I try to calm her down and get her
to back off and stop yelling at me.

One of my 'shoulds' that I am finding it hard to get rid of
is that I feel that when someone yells at me, I 'should' have
grown beyond my fear of anger that developed in
childhood. But the reality is that I cannot stand it when
people yell at me. Especially when all I am trying to do is
have an adult to adult conversation about something that
really has to change or we will never meet our deadline.

■ Childhood memories can still influence us

It does remind me of those childhood panics sitting on
the stairs hearing my mother and step-father shouting
abuse at each other. Hearing their accusations of each
others' wrongs, their naked hatred, their murderous
threats, I would sit paralysed, listening to the glass
breaking, stunned into a kind of catatonic waiting for
death to come.

My half-brothers would emerge from their rooms and we
would wait in total silence for the end of our world. We

would never talk about it then, or in the days that followed. Maybe the pain was too great to share. Maybe we had no language to express our feelings, no words that were adequate. Maybe to discuss it would be to make it too real to face.

We would have breakfast with glass on the kitchen floor and the morning cold creeping through the shattered door and window panes. The workman would arrive and ask us what happened.

'My dad couldn't get in,' says my younger brother.

'Did he need to break all the panes of glass in the door and the windows?' asks the man.

We are silent. We eat our cornflakes out of unfamiliar bowls. The others lie in pieces in the bin.

We dread going to school. Will the house be there when we return? Will there be anyone there to cook our tea? Will the world go on turning on its axis?

At school I retreat into my own world. The teacher smacks my hand for not listening. She moves me to the front and shouts at me. She fires a question at me, but I don't know the answer and she knows I don't know the answer. That is why she asks me.

I retreat further and further.

I do not cry because this happens to everyone. It is just how life is. I grit my teeth and float into my fantasy world where an imaginary parent encloses me with loving arms and I can fall asleep with some kind of certainty that the world will still be there when I awake.

■ Childhood fear and adult anger

Presumably for all of us, childhood held some kind of trauma:

■ the death of a beloved grandparent

■ the loss of a friend

■ accidents

■ the fact that the world is a frightening place when you are little and do not have the power to communicate your feelings and your needs.

So probably for all of us there are feelings that were so hard to deal with as children that we buried them, and they emerge in adulthood as inexplicable aspects of our lives, perhaps coming out as anger over some small thing.

I have come to see this anger at such little things as really about much deeper things within myself. These are shrouded in the mystery of forgotten childhood and it looks like a lifetime's work to understand them.

In the meantime, I try to watch for those little irritations that can spark off anger (I am sure that most people must have them), and try to make sure they do not get out of proportion. They can do that all too easily.

■ Recognizing our stress

We need to acknowledge our stresses and start to understand how things in our childhood might still be influencing us. Then we might be able to manage them more successfully. Here are some of mine I have listed over the past few months:

■ anxiety at the prospect of people coming for a meal or coming to stay

■ feeling there is too much to do at work and not enough time to do it

■ the panic feelings of Christmas

■ anxiety at planning a teaching session. (Will it be any good? Can I do it?)

If we really try to understand some of these sometimes unexpected anxieties, irritations and stresses, we might find that they shed some light on our real feelings deep inside. For me these include:

■ anger at being put down

- a desperate need not to be controlled by anyone else (a kind of rage overtakes me when people tell me that I 'should' do this, or I 'ought' to do that!)

- a fear of being with others and a need for personal space.

For you the things might be quite different.

As I listened to people talking about their low self-esteem, I could see that anger in some form or other was a common reaction. Understanding our anger is a part of understanding who we really are.

■ Self-harm

It must be a part of the anger that I see in so many people who are depressed or who have low self-esteem that we often seem to want to harm ourselves in some way. For me it is a quite straightforward wish to damage my body – cut my wrists, beat my head against a brick wall. Anything will do as long as I hurt myself. Stopping myself from doing it (which mostly now I can do) is quite a struggle. I can do it sometimes by escaping from where I am to somewhere else where I feel safe.

It is a curious thing, though. Something goes wrong and my reaction is to want to slash my wrists. It puzzles me why it is like that but I have seen it in others and maybe it is our need to destroy ourselves because we are bad? The need to hurt and be hurt? An escape from our overwhelming feelings?

The raging self-hatred bursts out of me sometimes. Now it is much less about the wish to die – though that returns when the dreaded depression descends on me like a cloud of swarming locusts darkening the sky and demolishing everything in their path. The self-hatred now seems much more to do with the feeling that I need to be punished, or that in some way I deserve to be hurt. If I do hurt myself, the feelings are incredibly complex. First, there is the dramatic relief. The pain brings a release of something – I don't know what.

Then I can cry both from the pain, the relief and – you guessed it – the terrible shame of what I have done. Somehow it must all be to do with anger, but that amount of anger scares me.

It is as if I had the power to blow up the world. But I must contain it within me. I must be bad because I am angry and I must be stupid to hurt myself, so where are you, God, in all this? Gone? Given up on me because I am so pathetic?

■ It is OK to be angry

I know in my head that it is OK to be angry. Many have tried to convince me that it is otherwise, but I am now firmly convinced that it is fine to feel anger. Anyway, there is nothing we can do about it. If we feel it, we feel it. That is all there is to it. The important thing then is not to go and murder someone, or take it out on someone else, or do anything else that is harmful.

There is fear that to release that much anger will be to cause some cataclysmic explosion that may rock the universe – well, my bit of it anyway. I know I am not up to what Superman can do, but it feels that powerful so maybe I have reason to feel so very afraid.

Who or what I am so afraid of I am not quite clear. Maybe it is a fear of myself. Maybe it is a fear of what others would say if I were to reveal my anger.

Anger is something I have been taught to be ashamed of.

■ What is behind our anger?

Lots of people say they feel like me, so what might be at the bottom of it?

For me I can make a direct link to my need as a child not to show any feelings at all. If I expressed dislike of something being done to me, or objected to something, then I would be punished. I soon learnt to keep silent!

In my childhood family, no one, absolutely no one was allowed to say that they were afraid or that they were hurting inside. Anger was a terrifying, but silent, creature. It destroyed, and went on destroying, in some insidious way long after the event.

It was never safe to feel anything, so I suppose I learnt to feel nothing.

Many of us failed to develop a good and healthy view of ourselves as children. Someone somewhere along the line was putting us down, bullying us, using us, and not taking care of us in the nurturing kind of way that all children need. So maybe we had to split our mind off from what was happening to us.

We might have told ourselves that:

■ parents are always right, they look after their children, so what is happening to me can't be really happening.

■ I will go into my own fantasy world where everything is OK.

■ I will assume it is me that is bad because parents are good and right.

■ I will totally forget all of this because it is too traumatic to think about.

Someone abuses us. We don't feel it. Someone abandons us (maybe through death or desertion). We don't dare let ourselves feel it.

We learn to feel nothing. We anaesthetize all our feelings and by the time we are adults we don't know how to feel things any longer. Except that every now and then, when we least expect it, feelings of depression, loneliness, desperation, guilt, and a total lack of value of ourselves crash into our life, wrecking it and bringing pain that we cannot relate to anything in our consciousness.

Positive Pointers

If we share our enthusiasm and our love with those around us they might want to be with us much more.

Learn to relax.

1. Start sharing positive information about yourself with those close to you.

2. Think about what Henry Ford said: 'There isn't a person anywhere that isn't capable of doing more than he thinks he can.'

9
Starting to Change

Every day in every way I get better and better.

I am not sure who said that truly awful saying, but I knew someone once who really believed in it. She was a nurse in a hospital in which there were about 50 of us supposed to be recovering from 'nervous breakdowns'. She used to wander around the ward exhorting us in her own special way, but to me it was all so clearly untrue (that I was getting better every day), that I found it rather alarming. Days, weeks and months were going by and it seemed to me that I was feeling worse.

'You have to change how you think', this nurse would say.

'Fine,' I'd think, 'but how exactly do I do that?'

This is the crunch. Yes. I was happy to see that something needed to change, but how? I had been thinking in my way for as long as I could remember – obviously! Telling me to change how I think is like telling me to change how I talk, change how I eat, change my favourite position to go to sleep and change how I walk. Yes. It might be possible to change these things, I suppose, but only with a huge amount of difficulty. I don't think I can do it. It is completely overwhelming.

So I more or less rejected this kind of exhortative therapy. It seemed mindless, stupid, wrong and proved conclusively, once and for all, that everyone else might be able to change the way they think, but not me, because I am hopeless and useless.

■ Change is complex

Change is possible, but very complex. It goes in fits and starts, but it is happening. Most important of all, it takes a great deal of time. That is why I suggested you make this into a rainbow book and keep coming back to it over several years.

Much of this book is about that process of change I am experiencing and that others have told me about in their lives. Most people told me that they thought they were 'growing' – becoming more confident and more able to manage life. Others, especially those who were in the depths of depression, were unable to point to any change or any hope of change, but I think that was the depression talking. When you are in the very depths of depression, the thought of life being any different is impossible.

■ Life gets better

Over months and years our lives can change, but it is very hard work. No, I should rephrase that and be a bit more honest! It is painstaking, gruelling and at times a discouraging slog. Many times I just sit, exhausted, and cry for the sheer frustration of it.

■ What to expect as you explore your lack of self-esteem

> **It is our failure to understand ourselves which causes most of our suffering.**
>
> Dorothy Rowe

People who have told me about their low self-esteem say that by starting to understand their low self-esteem and by doing something about it, they can at least start to understand their feelings a bit more. One of the main purposes of this book is for you to try to gain some of that insight into what makes you tick. As well as working on the book, you might want to keep a journal and/or talk to someone about what you are thinking and learning.

■ Keeping a journal

It isn't essential to keep a journal, but people who do often find it helpful – even if they hardly ever write in it. One sentence, once a month, telling ourselves about what we are feeling and any progress we might be making is very much better than nothing at all. It is the start of our being determined to understand ourselves better.

Therapy was the beginning of those personal insights for me. At least I could try to search for the right questions to ask about why I found life such a trial. (I wanted instant answers, of course – I still do – but answers take some time to develop, if they come at all. Most of us have to be content at first with finding the right questions.)

It was the untangling of some of those feelings that has so helped me to feel a little better about myself – I am hesitating writing that sentence! I am not sure it is true to say that I feel better about myself, at least, not all the time. What is true is that therapy has helped me to understand what I am thinking and feeling for at least some of the time. Even one disastrous group therapy I entered did in the end teach me something about myself. This included the rather alarming thought that I could quite easily have murdered the therapist, such was my anger with her!

If your search for some kind of personal meaning is like mine, it is likely to include times of great excitement and exhilaration, but other times of furious rage and murderous hate! It is OK to feel all that stuff – just don't act on it, OK?

■ Suicidal feelings

Some of the rage and hate could be about people you think hurt you, but some of it is likely to be self-hatred. This is a huge part of low self-esteem for many people. My logical reaction to my intense self-hatred is to want to die. I tried to get off this funny little planet several times, but failed. But now I can hardly express my thankfulness that I did fail. My self-hatred and suicidal feelings have changed (they have not gone away) into gratitude that now I have learnt to live my life reasonably happily. I now know what I would have done to my family if I had succeeded. I thought they would all be better off without me, but I was utterly, completely and devastatingly wrong about that. I cry just to think about what I might have done to hurt them. People I know who have had to survive the suicide of a friend or family member have had their world utterly shattered.

■ If you are one of those many people who think that life is too much of a struggle, **PLEASE** stick with life.

■ It might take a long time, but those feelings can and do change. The chance of failure in suicide attempts is quite high and we risk life as a brain-damaged 'vegetable'.

■ Talk to someone.

■ Tell your doctor.

■ If you live in Britain, the Samaritans are always at the end of the phone.

■ Read more of this book and keep telling yourself that many people who feel suicidal go on to have enormous gratitude that they somehow got through that stage.

■ Living more at peace with ourselves

Several people I talked to seemed to be saying that raising their self-esteem was about living more at peace with themselves and having some kind of inner contentment.

That makes sense.

There are no requirements for starting out on the task of finding a place of inner peace and contentment within ourselves except that:

■ you have to want to change.

■ the only person who can make a difference to your problems in life is you – but don't give up! You started this book exactly because you want to do something about your life!

So – go for it.

We *can* change.

We *can* build up our self-esteem.

We *can* change the quality of our life.

Activity

1. We have to be able to rest and feel safe behind our wall and have times to be alone and meditate. Giving ourselves time to reflect on our life (and perhaps to write in our journal) is crucial if we are to grow as people.

2. If there are a lot of people in your house, find a way to tell them that you need this time, maybe when you sit in a special chair, or a particular time of the day when they know not to bother you. If all else fails, shut yourself in the loo and play loud music to blot out their enraged cries.

3. I used this activity in my depression book, but it can be such a helpful one that I have included it here as well. Write your own obituary. However, before you do that, think how Princess Diana would have written her obituary. People who knew her said she would have had no idea that people loved her so much.

It is quite likely that those who know you think very much more positively about you than you do yourself, so write it in a very upbeat way.

Princess Diana had very low self-esteem. She needed reassurance all the time… She would have had no idea that at her death there would have been this great outpouring of grief. She would have been surprised.

Rosa Monkton, Diana's friend

Part 4

Looking at Life Beyond the Wall

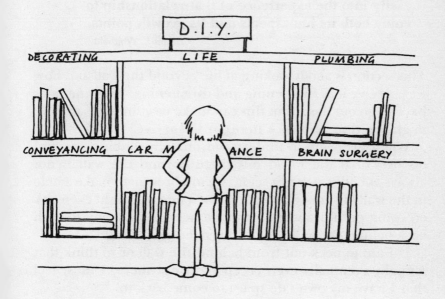

10
Making Clear Boundaries

> A key to having healthy boundaries is flexibility
> and adaptability. When we are able to be flexible
> and adaptable in any relationship – without being
> mistreated or abused – we can know ourselves in
> a deeper and richer way. And we can let go more
> easily into the experience of that relationship to
> enjoy both its fun aspects and its growth points.
>
> Charles L. Whitfield

This section is about looking at life beyond the wall and how
we perceive it as frightening and threatening. We sometimes
have to go out there, but this can make us vulnerable and we
might need to rush back in order to survive.

When we begin to understand ourselves a bit more and
discover that the world out there beyond the wall is not
always as bad as it might seem, we might want to make a hole
in the wall big enough to peep out. Then we might even risk
creeping out for a while – but we need to be ready to rush
back behind the wall when things get too difficult!

If I am to peek out from behind the wall or to think that
I might eventually even creep right out there, I must feel
that I have my own safe space to come back to.

Life is frightening. So making sure that we have a completely
safe space, that is our own and that no one else invades, is very
important for our personal growth and well-being.

So our brick wall (that we might well have made into a
very secure tower by now) needs to be quite separate and
distinct from everybody else's space around us. We need our
absolutely safe space with a good stretch of neutral territory
between our space and the spaces around us.

■ Negotiating our own space

I think one of the reasons I have a good quality of life is because my family are very good at giving me space whenever I need it, even if that need comes suddenly and unpredictably. I could not stay in a relationship that didn't give me space.

We all need to negotiate with those around us in order to make sure that we have our own space which no one else invades. Relationships can feel very crowded sometimes, and if people come into our space and trample all over us, we can feel uncomfortable. This is a sign that we need to be a bit more assertive and ask for some more personal space.

We need to think about what we need in terms of our personal boundaries and lay down some markers to prevent ourselves being invaded. Of course, any of us might want people in our personal space from time to time, but we want it when we want it, not when we don't, and that needs negotiating.

■ Free to be intimate

Intimacy of any kind is fine if we want it at that time. If we don't, it can be hell, and getting our relationships healthy, open, real, and negotiated is a crucial aspect of improving our life for the better.

It is when I have a clear boundary around me that I can be free to be intimate. A boundary does not need to cut me off from those around me – though I might choose that. It is this clarity about my space that means that I can have relationships with others who are, hopefully, clear about their space.

With my clear boundaries I am free to:

■ love.

■ have my own beliefs and disagree with others if I want to.

■ be assertive and be clear about what I really want.

■ be myself.

- **withdraw when I need to.**

- **decide on the level of physical contact I want.**

- **express my anger and frustration.**

- **change as a person.**

- **take risks.**

I do not expect to be:

- **betrayed.**

- **rejected.**

- **manipulated.**

- **abused in any way.**

But if that does happen, I can renegotiate and build the trust back up again – hopefully!

■ Being assertive

Being assertive and saying what I want and need is not being selfish, it is being real. If I can make it clear what my needs are, I am being genuine about my inner life. If I say what I want, I share a bit of myself with you, I take the risk of being open and I let you discover who I am.

Of course I must be sensitive in that process to the needs of others. Of course I must not keep insisting that everything that goes on in the relationship is only built around my needs – that would make it a rather unhealthy relationship.

But,

- **the meek woman who lets her husband make all the decisions**

- **the shy person who would rather put up with what they don't want than share their real thinking**

■ the person who lets another in the relationship make all the running and take all the responsibility,

these people are not taking their share of the practicalities of any relationship.

■ Signs of invaded boundaries

The things which show that our boundaries need more negotiating are things such as:

■ our sense that we just don't get enough time to be ourselves.

■ any sense that we are carrying too much of the responsibility for the relationship, for example always being the one who makes the family meal.

■ a parent who treats their children as an extension of themselves and expects the child to do and be exactly what the parent wants.

■ abuse in a relationship.

■ a family in which one or more members keeps feeling responsible for other people's feelings.

■ A relationship in which there is a great deal of acted-out anger.

■ A relationship in which our feelings are not given enough value; for example we need to have time to grieve in our own way, adolescents need to be able to grow within a family that will understand and be tolerant. We need to be accepted for who we are and not labelled by our parents, for example, 'Tom's our shy one, and Eddie is our naughty one.'

■ Any relationship or family in which each member is not given sufficient privacy – even the smallest child needs their own physical space, to be allowed to have secrets, and be given time just to 'be'.

■ Setting boundaries

If we are in some kind of unhealthy relationship, we must try to renegotiate our boundaries if we are to survive and if we are to value the other people in the relationship.

These are examples of unhealthy boundaries that need to be reset:

- the young woman who keeps ending up with unsuitable partners.

- the young man who feels that his mother is hanging on to him in an unhealthy way.

- the daughter who feels that whatever she does for her mother, she is never thanked or shown any gratitude.

- the person in a relationship in which they are constantly told they 'should do this' and they 'ought to do that'.

- anyone in a manipulative relationship.

- anyone in what Americans call co-dependent relationships, that is each sustaining the other in unhelpful rather than helpful ways.

- the young person who feels that his parents are still far too protective and intrusive and still treat him like a child.

- the boss at work who is overdemanding.

- the colleague at work who flirts.

It is not easy to negotiate some change in a relationship, that we want and need, but if we don't, we will have to put up with things that we need not. We risk not being able to nurture our inner life and grow as people.

■ Walls do not make ideal boundaries

When we are negotiating boundaries in a relationship we will always want to build in flexibility.

- Some days I might just be too tired to make the decision about what would be best and I would rather you just decided.

- Some days I might want to sit up close to you or hug you, but other days I might not.

■ **Some days I might lose my cool and throw a complete strop, but I will not be expecting you to reject me, or remove your love.**

Walls are a bit too inflexible for this! But if we need our wall, that is fine for now. It keeps us safe. It helps us to feel at peace with ourselves at least some of the time. It can help us to be in touch with our inner life. But we will be working our way towards creeping out some of the time.

Positive Pointers

Nurturing those around you, smiling, being kind and caring enough to think of the needs of others are all ways to start to feel good about yourself.

Keep your attitude positive. That way you learn from your mistakes and turn them into learning experiences.

Activity

1. Write in your journal about times when you feel (or felt) as if your space is invaded.

2. Think through any unhealthy relationship you are in. Does it need some renegotiating of the boundaries?

3. Start a 'happy book' – a small notebook that you are only allowed to write happy and positive thoughts in. Mine is a fluffy one with Tigger (Pooh's friend) on the cover and when you press Tigger's nose he sings a song – but any pretty notebook will do.

11
Peeping Out

> **We are secure. God is running the show. Neither our feelings of depression nor the facts of suffering... are evidence that God has abandoned us.**
>
> Eugene Paterson

Out there beyond the wall, life is tough. The world is full of horrible things: people who kill and hurt children, corrupt police officers, people who put their own lifestyle before caring for our planet, slot machines in arcades by the sea, nylon bedsheets, other people's loud radios, newspapers that spread gossip, slugs, crowded smoky waiting rooms, people who sit on the underground train cracking the joints in their fingers, people entering into the Guinness Book of Records for being able to eat louder than anyone else, people who put their chewing gum on the ground so that it gets stuck to my shoe, and meetings where there is tea and coffee, but not nearly enough chocolate biscuits.

Maybe the sound of eating does not make you feel you want to rush from the room screaming hysterically like it does me. What one person can tolerate, another can't.

■ Life is tough for everyone

But if we are able to see that life is tough, and are able to work out which things are hard for us (so best avoided or gone through with our defences up and a firm grip on our teddy bear), then we know that we are making progress. We can peep out and look at it all, and see that life is tough for everyone. Some people might find it a bit easier than us, but there are others who find it at least as tough as we do.

We have probably all met at least one person who gives out the strong message that life is one long party. Nothing bothers them (so they say). Never had a day of depression in their life (so they say). Life is for living. (Why do people say that? I get an overwhelming desire to smack their face.)

I wonder if some of those people who say they can handle everything are so heavily fortified by their tower and any other defences they can muster that they are not really connecting with their feelings. These people can be loud and brash – and sometimes utterly obnoxious. I like to think that if we admit we find life tough, we are being much more honest. We acknowledge that our feelings are all over the place, that we are hurting and that life outside the tower is terrifying. So we can picture ourselves peeping out of our tower and know that we have got past the first hurdle. At least we see the reality of life – it is tough and often inexplicable. Our task now is to find ways to cope with it.

◼ Advice we are given

We can listen to advice, but it will not necessarily help immediately or even at all. People have been telling me for years that I need to become more thick-skinned. 'What you need to do is develop a hide like a rhinoceros', they say. Over the years, I think about it. I see that I am much too sensitive. But is the way out of it to try to be immune to what life throws at me? Might that also mean I could lose my ability to empathize and recognize pain in others?

I say this, of course, because despite trying desperately hard to simulate rhinoceros hide, I fail drastically – so I tell myself that it probably wouldn't be for the best anyway!

◼ Assertiveness training

Yes. Lots of people have said this to me and it is probably a good idea. Each year I look at the classes in the local adult education brochure. But I am not yet assertive enough to decide to enrol, so I don't. I have tried a few books with varying success. I went to one session at an arts festival in a huge tent with about a hundred others. I ended up in tears and could not cope with the rest of the day. I know I am more assertive than I was 10 years ago and this is an area in which I need to grow more – just like many people I know, especially women.

Many people have changed their ways of thinking and behaving through going to classes, so that might be a good way forward for you.

■ Count your blessings

My problems with facing life are probably insignificant compared with the people on the television news last week who were tearing at the rubble after an earthquake, their fingers bleeding as their digging gets more frantic to find a missing loved one. Or the street children in South America who have no one to put their arms around them and reassure them of love. I have so much more than they do. In comparison with their pain, mine seems trivial.

So then I hate myself for feeling it. I have a loving partner, two fabulous children, a warm and comfortable home, a job, so why does it matter that inside I am crying?

I don't know.

■ Comparing pain

Perhaps human pain is not something we can compare from one person to the next. It is neither less than nor more than anyone else's. I have seen people refuse to look at their pain and let themselves see that they are really hurting, by saying that it is nothing like the pain in some other people or in a country far away. This can be a way of denying the strength of our feelings.

Of course we want to give help to those who suffer in war and famine. Of course I can hardly imagine what it would be like to be unable to feed my children because there has been no rain and no harvest. But I don't think you can compare pain. For all of us, our pain is *our pain* and that is what we try to overcome within ourselves.

When we peep out from behind our wall, we need to keep telling ourselves that it is tough out there for everyone.

Positive Pointer

The time *will* come when you will feel ready to get out there beyond the wall.

Activity

Assertiveness is quite different from aggressiveness and we will need to work hard at seeing that difference – especially if we are nervous about being assertive and then that makes us come over as being more aggressive than we mean to be.

The main things I have learnt about needing to be more assertive are:

■ making sure I put my point clearly and concisely

■ making it very clear what I want and need and why

■ making sure the other person really does 'hear' me

■ practising what I want to say in front of the mirror first

■ not getting into the negative 'stuff' like 'You always…' and 'You never…' but staying positive

■ acting confidently – even if I don't feel that way

■ keeping my cool no matter what

■ remaining polite but firm if they do the angry alligator bit – and then just walk away.

Go for it! It all sounds much harder than it actually is.

12
Shifting the First Stone

What is this force that pushes us as individuals and as a whole species to grow against the natural resistance of our own lethargy? It is love.

M. Scott Peck

One of the things that a surprising number of people told me about their low self-esteem is the enormous amount of fear they experience and their very sensitive reactions to difficult or critical situations. I found this very reassuring because it meant that I am not alone in my fear and sensitivity.

Unless we are going to give in to our fear and sensitivity completely and for ever, we need to think about overcoming that fear and shifting the first stone in the wall and at least consider living even for a short while beyond the wall. If we can do that this time, maybe we will be able to do it again.

■ Fear and sensitivity

I am too frightened to look at the news. The guns, tanks and crying children frighten me. The images have been coming back in my nightmares for several days. I try the radio news, but there are in-depth interviews about rape, murder and violence. I decide to give up on news for now. I will have to make do with reading other people's newspapers on the bus going to work. I am getting good at swivelling my eyeballs around so that I can make sense of the headlines.

It seems that it is common not to have the confidence to deal with what life throws at us, but it is much more than that. We live with an inner dread of life that can develop into an all-consuming terror. These feelings can easily overwhelm us.

■ Different kinds of fear

Fear is quite a complex thing. Some people seem to enjoy watching horror movies. I freak out if I see a trailer of one! All of us would feel some kind of fear if we were, for example, told that the plane we are in is going to crashland; or we watch the news and hear that there is a train crash and we know a loved one was travelling by train that day.

The 'ordinary everyday fear' we might have can vary from person to person. To some people, going out of the house, ringing someone up, telling someone something they won't want to hear, or joining a group is not probably that difficult. But for some of us, it is things like that we just cannot face.

Then there is what I will call 'real' fear of doing dangerous things. I love putting myself into some dangerous situations such as going up a rock face, squirming down a very narrow pothole, and leaping across a torrent of water in the Yorkshire Dales. I have a huge desire to jump out of an aeroplane (parachute in working order, I hope). Some people I know simply cannot understand me wanting to do this kind of thing, so fear must have some very different meanings for people.

But again, some people would cope with that real fear much more calmly than others. The real fear I cannot cope with at all is being in a situation of conflict, or any situation where I feel I am in sexual danger such as in a train carriage at night with just one man.

Finding ways, gradually, to build up our self-confidence, to face our fears, to try to overcome them, seems to me to be a major part of being willing to shift the first few stones and consider living beyond the wall.

■ Panic attacks

I feel that I cannot face it any more. The feelings engulf me to the point where I feel I can hardly breathe. Inside me my heart pounds and the blood pulses through my brain so loudly I cannot hear properly. I think I will be sick. I try some deep breathing.

My fear mounts as the feelings keep bombarding me. I then have a choice. I know from experience that if I can get myself into a totally different situation and find some personal space, I might be able to calm down. I also know that I can make myself stick it out. I can force myself to turn my back on the fear and get on with what I am doing anyway and just believe that the fear will go away.

It is tough to do that. It leaves me exhausted to the point where I cannot think straight and I do not have the co-ordination even to press the right buttons to make a phone call. But if I do sit it out I try to keep telling myself that I did it. That I turned my back on the fear and the feelings and I achieved something.

■ Do not push too much

I have pushed myself too much recently and I know I need to take time off or I will crack up. It is hard to do that though because I will feel a failure and when I bury myself in my work it helps me to escape from the horrors of the thoughts inside my head and the fear that holds me in its icy grip. It is work that I use to keep myself safe behind my brick wall. But, of course, to work I need to meet others so I must face that world of fear beyond the wall.

As a tactic for surviving life, surrounding myself with work and pushing myself through the fear can be counter-productive, because when I get to the point of total exhaustion I can't work at all and I am a crumpled heap alone with my thoughts and the very fear I was trying to escape.

Learning to deal with our fear is one of the most crucial aspects of living with ourselves out there beyond the wall.

■ Pushing enough to get the buzz

Just because we feel terrified of doing something, it doesn't mean that we shouldn't do it. Pushing ourselves too far isn't wise, but the way I see it, if I don't push myself rather often, how would I know when I am pushing too much? It is all too easy to tell myself that I cannot manage it. If we are to make progress, sometimes inevitably we will push ourselves too much. I force myself to do something every now and then and I get such a buzz out of that. I did it. I didn't think I could but I did! (Time for chocolate.)

■ Giving in

If I give in to my fear it can make it all the worse because then I have not only my fear, but also my sense of uselessness that I could not cope. If I let my nervousness win today, it could mean that I won't make the phone call or go out of the house tomorrow either. Logically it follows that I may never pick up the phone ever again!

I could spend the rest of my life never going out of the house and although that superficially feels good, I know it would not work because of the sense of isolation.

A sense of frustration came through as I talked with people about low self-esteem. We cannot face going for a more demanding job, or visiting a relative we have been avoiding, or doing whatever it is that we feel is too hard, but the implications of letting our fear win every time is scary.

I know from past experience that if I give in to the fears all the time and keep behind the brick wall, my fears just multiply in my mind. I end up in that confusing dark world where there are ogres at every turn and everything that happens is a waking nightmare of ghouls and monsters. I have lived in that world for months at a time in the past and I have no wish to go back there.

Equally, if I face the fear and just do it every time, or even most of the time, I end up a quivering wreck!

■ Feel the fear and do it anyway

Susan Jeffers in her wonderful book *Feel the Fear and Do It Anyway* seems to be saying that we must get out there and do it – whatever the challenge. But I think we just *cannot do that all the time*. If we are:

- depressed, or

- at the very early stages of trying to face up to our inner fear, or

- at any kind of 'emergency stage' in dealing with our emotions (such as memories from childhood abuse coming back) and we are finding it hard just to deal with ordinary life,

then we need to be kind to ourselves, and not always make ourselves 'just do it anyway'.

■ Valuing ourselves for who we are

Yes, we might feel some sense of failure if we have to give in, but we need to consider sometimes why it is so important to us to 'just do it'. I know that often I 'just do it' because when I achieve things I feel better about myself. I do tend to value myself *only* through what I *achieve*. That can be very unhealthy because then I do not value myself for *who I am*.

But, having said that, if we do achieve something, we need to let ourselves feel really good about it. My friend managed to get herself back to teaching adults after years of finding difficulty with any kind of more pressurized work like that. She overcame her fear (with great difficulty) and now she is rightly proud of herself for what she has done.

She had moved a stone in her wall. She overcame her fear. Now she feels stronger and values herself both for what she did, and for the lovely person that she is.

■ What if...?

I am a terrible 'what-ifer'. What if one of my children was to die? This is so terrifying that I cannot even think about it without feeling the fear and the tears. If my partner is half an hour late home, I am picturing him dead under a bus and I am waiting for the police at the door. What if...? What if...? This fantasy fear is crippling my life. If I keep on like this, I will worry all my life and keep myself unhappy, in a

043557

high state of crippling anxiety, exactly the conditions for a stroke or heart failure.

As someone once said, 'I've had a lot of worries in my life but most of them never happened.' I know I am letting 'what ifs' dominate my life.

'What ifs' can trap us in a state of constant worry and shut behind the wall. But we can learn from them. It is as if facing our greatest fears can make us a bit stronger.

So, some 'what ifs' could be OK. The ones to learn to walk away from are those that mean you are not enjoying today because of the fears of tomorrow.

Positive Pointers

You *do* have inner personal power to overcome fear. You can use that power gradually to develop your own strategies for being brave enough to make a tiny hole in the wall.

If you manage to shift just one stone a bit and just creep out into the world a little, the sense of success you feel is amazing. But you need not to stay out there too long. Get back behind the wall quickly and tell yourself you did it.

Activity

1. Try to list your 'what ifs'. Try to see if there are some that are keeping you gripped in fantasy fear.

2. What could you plan for to try to keep these fears in their place?

3. What could you do to move your first stone?

13
Living as Misfits

No one is useless in this world who lightens the burdens of another.

Charles Dickens

If we have moved a stone and are to trying to live the other side of the wall at least some of the time, there are likely to be times when we will feel we don't quite fit in the world. I feel this quite frequently and many of the people I talked to said, 'People find me odd.'

So maybe the feeling that we are misfits in our society is just one of those odd feelings that many humans get. Perhaps this is something that goes along with low self-esteem; something about our culture and the focus on individualism.

■ Doing odd things

I think it is best to think of life as such a thing of mystery that much of it is not going to make sense. For example, I do the most odd things.

■ I talk to myself. (That is partly why I like to have a dog because I can pretend I am talking to her.) But if you look at people in cars, many are either talking or singing to themselves.

■ I have my own fantasy world which is so much more interesting than what some people call the 'real' world, so I stay in it for large amounts of time. It keeps my life bearable.

■ I hang up my jeans where I can see them every day to remind myself that I am hoping one day to get them on. Then I eat a whole packet of chocolate biscuits and am not sure why I did it. I look at the jeans. Then I hate myself.

And so on.

I found out that many people do odd things like I do so maybe I am not the crazy, madwoman I sometimes think I am. It seems that to live more peaceably with ourselves, we need gradually to learn to accept ourselves as we are. Life, the world and the universe is such a mystery, that not really understanding it, and feeling 'odd', seems to be just how it is.

■ Accepting ourselves

I can see that I might never be able to handle life as well as some people seem to. It might seem easy to go at life more gently and pace myself, but it doesn't seem to be my style. I tell myself how stupid I am. How difficult can it be to learn to relax and go gently? So I try again – and just fail. I have this plan that I will stop in the middle of every day and relax for five minutes. You would think that would be a fairly easy thing to do, wouldn't you?

We can want to change some things (lose that excess weight, get fitter, get out there and do something with our lives), but we need to learn to distinguish between the things that we can change and those we cannot. (We will come back to this later.) I used to try to change things I couldn't. That is incredibly stupid.

What I mean here is working towards:

■ the feeling about ourselves that we are OK.

■ feeling at peace with ourselves as we are.

■ learning to smile at ourselves.

■ trying to block out the negative 'old tapes' and give ourselves more positive messages; for example, instead of, 'I'm a misfit', we could say, 'I'm a unique person with my own quirky humour and an off-the-wall view of life and I don't want to be a conforming person anyway. This is just the way I am.' Then see if you can add, 'And I like me the way I am.' (Tough one.)

■ Pirouetting with eggs

Outside the wall we are going to have to learn to live with misunderstandings. One of the things I have been learning about in the last 10 years is that I often misunderstand situations or what people mean by what they say and write. I think misunderstandings could be, for many of us, part of why we disappeared behind the wall in the first place.

This morning my daughter is packing up her boxes to go back to college. As I was ironing, I noticed on the side of a box (obviously used to transport eggs to shops) the sentence, 'Sell your eggs in rotation.'

I immediately had a mental picture of shopkeepers in little pink tutus, pirouetting around in tight circles to the music of the sugar-plum fairy and selling eggs to surprised customers. I think I can be reasonably sure that is not quite the intended meaning of advice on how to sell eggs.

I was thinking about this as I ironed and realized I am probably misunderstanding my therapist Ruth at the moment. I am terribly angry with her and feel that I have lost my trust in her. As I wrote about it in a torrent of fury in my journal this morning, I could only see the anger. Now, I can see that if I made the effort, summoned up more courage and talked to her about it, it is quite likely to be a case of pirouetting with eggs. What she meant is probably not what I thought she meant. The real meaning got lost somewhere on its journey from her brain to mine.

■ Misunderstandings happen all the time

There was a bug somewhere in the system. (So you see, I am saying to myself as I write this, 'You are a hopeless and useless person and you can't even listen to someone properly, and all this worry has been about nothing. You are such a fool', etc.) OK. I can try not to blame myself.

But the crucial thing to learn is that misunderstandings probably happen all the time. Instead of going off in a huff when someone in my family says something to me that I am upset by, I try now to get clarity of what they meant. I am astonished how often I get it wrong and get all steamed up thinking they are putting me down, when all the time their meaning was quite different.

It is just too easy to think you understand something when you don't. And furthermore, when there is another level of meaning, things can take on subtleties that in our defensive state behind the wall, we don't always see.

■ Looking at a deeper level

Take patchwork, for example. When I explain what I do in patchwork, I can see people's eyes glazing over and giving me that look of wonderment that any human being with any sense would want to spend hours cutting up material into little bits and then sewing them all back together again. I can see why people think it is crazy. What I need to do is also to communicate to them what is going on at a much deeper level: the amazing thrill of the mathematical patterns, the blending of colours, and the sheer joy of creating beauty.

As I go through this time-consuming activity along with all the back pain and the frustration, as I am making a quilt, I am thinking almost all the time of the person I am making it for and how much I love them. I see this as a kind of prayer.

So if people don't see what is going on at this deeper level, they will not see the great meaning that patchwork has for me. What it looks like at first glance (chopping up and sewing back together again) is not even close to what is really going on in the deeper world of love and creativity.

■ We can get it wrong

It can be like this when bad things happen to us. We think we understand what people say and do, but often we have missed the point completely. Understanding what people mean in their words and actions is a very delicate and confusing thing. From where I am sitting in my tower, I am realizing more and more that I often get it drastically wrong.

■ You are special

Another aspect of dealing with our fears that we don't seem to fit into the world is to learn to give ourselves much more significance.

I went to see my osteopath yesterday. It is an expensive business, but the relief from the pain is so wonderful that it is worth every penny. I have also found that osteopaths can be very wise and sensitive people who can treat physical well-being in a way that can be much better than traditional Western medicine.

Yesterday we were talking about self-esteem and I was explaining how I can't do this book because I don't feel OK about myself. All the time I feel a hypocrite to be writing it and I feel too hopeless a person to be trying to do such a hard task.

Robin looked at me and said, 'But you're special. Everyone is special, aren't they?' He suggested I try to tell myself that I am special, so I did. I sat on the train going home and said it a few times to myself and I felt all warm inside. I knew I was sitting there with a silly grin on my face! It felt so good!

Everyone is a unique creation (unless you are Dolly the cloned sheep, so let us hope ideas of cloning humans don't get too far off the starting blocks). So however much we have been brainwashed to believe we are hopeless and useless individuals, that just isn't true.

Positive Pointers

We are all unique.

We are all special.

We all have value.

1. Tell yourself that you are special. (I have found that it is easier to believe that some days than others.) Everyone is special and can make a difference to their life by believing it. This is what gives us the power to shift a few bricks and dare to get out there beyond the wall.

2. Try to ask for clarification next time you feel put down or annoyed. It has taken me years of practice to get started on this, so it is another one of those lifelong skills to develop.

3. Think carefully about your 'old tapes' and negative thinking that is all about past wounds. All that 'stuff' needs to be understood as the stuff that chains us to the wall. We need to find the key to those fetters before we have any chance of surviving out there beyond the wall.

4. Write about your 'stuff' and find someone trustworthy to talk to about it if you can.

14
Overcoming the Lies

**If we do not consciously and consistently focus
on the spiritual part of ourselves, we will never
experience the kind of joy, satisfaction and
connectedness we are all seeking.**

Susan Jeffers

Another feature of life outside the wall is that we are likely
to survive better if we are able to contradict the lies that we
were told about ourselves in the past.

For most of the people I talked to, their low self-esteem
has arisen out of things in their past. For example, as I have
said, many people were told at school that they are hopeless
at maths. I was told that over and over again, but now I find
maths utterly fascinating. I love it. I sit and doodle with
maths ideas on the train creating patterns and thinking
about numbers.

So I overcame the lie that I am no good at maths. There
are many things I still don't understand and I still panic
about, such as calculating something in front of someone
else, but now I can see that my being 'hopeless' was more to
do with bad teaching and my unwillingness to listen at
school (because it was boring compared with the interesting
things going on in my head).

■ We can overcome the lies

Because I overcame that lie, I can see that it must be possible
to overcome other lies.

Some of the lies we learnt have taught us to fear and to
fail and, most important, *to accept* our feelings of fear and
failure far too easily. There are some things we need to

accept because we cannot change them. We need to learn to see what we can change and distinguish it from things we can't. (This is a crucial life skill and something we will keep coming back to.) But crucially, we need to tell ourselves often that change does happen.

■ Will I be able to change?

Change both within organizations and within people is always slow, usually difficult, and is often done with conflict and tears. It is exhausting and can take all the strength and courage we can muster. But we can do it. I know I have changed just in the last year. When I look back over the five years of my therapy, I see considerable change – though it can come unhinged rather dramatically if I get into a situation I cannot handle. But I can get myself together again reasonably quickly now. What might have knocked me out for several hours can now be coped with in a few minutes. What used to send me into deep panic or depression for months can now be coped with in a few weeks. I can take a deep breath and carry on.

■ We are changing all the time

Sometimes talking to depressed people, they say they don't think they will be able to change at all. But we do all change throughout our life. It is just that sometimes it is so slow we hardly see it. However, change is something we also fear – rightly. Any change is a life event and if we are already overwhelmed by our struggle with low self-esteem, adding something else to our lives doesn't look like a good idea.

But to improve the quality of our lives, some kind of very slow change is really going to help us. If we go at it gently we can get there and it need not be that painful if we treat ourselves kindly and reward ourselves.

■ Rewarding ourselves

It is very important that we stop and tell ourselves we have done something well and have a reward.

One of the rewards I give myself is to go on patchwork courses, and last week when I went to one I learnt an important lesson in self-esteem. I was saying how I cannot get the points of my triangles right when I sew them. Another woman on the course, who was a patchwork expert, pointed out to me that since I had just bought a quarter-inch patchwork foot for my sewing machine, if I cut out the fabric carefully, then sewed a quarter-inch seam, I would get them much better.

I realized immediately what I was doing. I was *assuming* that because it was *me* doing it, any difficult bits I did would be badly done. I decided there and then to be more accurate and, most important, *I would believe I could do it accurately*.

So now I try to start with the assumption that I can do it accurately and get it right – and I do!

Positive Pointers

We need to believe we can do it.

Sometimes just stopping completely for a few minutes can make all the difference to our lives. We can meditate on something beautiful or restful and just let ourselves sense the peace and joy that can be ours.

Activity

This activity is one that I see as my life's work!

1. List the lies you were told about yourself. There could be dozens. I found it helpful to put a little comment after each one. (Then in my journal I rage about some of them at great length. No one else is going to read it, so I can be utterly brutal. This is disconcertingly pleasing in a rather uncomfortable way.)

Here are some of the lies I was told which may help you to get you started:

■ I am no use and will never come to anything.

■ I am a hopeless person.

Some of the 'lies we are told' are not actually spoken words. 'Lies' can come through actions as well. If we are treated as if we don't matter, we believe we don't matter.

2. Then try to complete the sentences below. As with everything else you try in this book, this is something to come back to again and again with your different coloured pens. It can help to date what you write. That way you see progress. Don't worry if the years pass by and you seem to be standing still with some things. That is just how life is and it is certainly not a sign of our failure. Change is very hard for every human being that ever lived.

■ In 10 years I would like to be... (Just one thing that you really would like to change in your life. Make sure it is something it is possible to change! It is likely to be something you will need help with.)

■ By next year I would like to be... (This could be something you will need a bit of help with.)

■ By the end of next month... (Keep it small!)

■ By next week I think I could... (Just one, simple, achievable thing.)

You could put this list where you can see it if you want and give yourself stars when you achieve something. (I know it sounds stupid, but a star chart works wonders for me.)

On Saturdays we don't do anything much, which is brilliant, and most weeks we go to church on Sunday. I wouldn't like to live without a spiritual element in my life. I have to make a connection.

Victoria Wood

15
Responsibility and Failure

What we live we learn. What we learn we practise. What we practise we become. What we become has consequences.

Dr Desmond Kelly, anxiety and depression expert

One of the crippling things that seems to happen to some people who have a difficult childhood, or have some other traumatic event that changes their life and thought processes significantly, is that as adults we can be inappropriately dependent on other people. It is not always inappropriate to be dependent on others; for example if we are injured we let the doctors and nurses take charge. But, if we depend on others too much and refuse to take responsibility for ourselves, that is a mega-serious problem.

We need to take responsibility for ourselves if we are to cope out there beyond the wall.

We tend to:

■ say, 'She made me angry,' when we need to take responsibility for our own feelings and reactions.

■ think, 'I can't do anything to make my life any better.' (Yes, we can.)

■ believe it was all someone else's fault. (It might have been, but we need to get beyond that.)

■ believe that bad things which have happened to us happened because we deserve nothing better and it was some kind of punishment. (Bad things happen to anybody irrespective of what we do or who we are.)

■ ask, 'What should I do now?' (We need to be working towards making up our own mind.)

■ Taking responsibility for our failures

Failure is fine if we can blame it on someone else. If we can see our failure as all 'her fault' or 'because of the way I was treated at school' or whatever, we will live an angry life, blaming failure onto anyone but ourselves.

Don't get me wrong here. Much of our life is so fundamentally an outcome of past things that often factors in the difficulties of our lives now are because of things that are in the past – often things that we had very little control over. BUT...

We must learn to take responsibility for our lives now although it can be excruciating if we know that any failure is at least something to do with some shortcoming in ourselves. We feel no good. Hopeless. A loser.

What people call 'failures' obviously will vary from person to person. In my years living in Oxford, several young students tragically killed themselves; sometimes they were not even getting 'B' grades and they had gone through school getting mostly 'A's. They interpreted their lower marks as 'failure'.

These young people were probably thought a great success by their families, but could not see that we cannot all fly high all of the time. They were captured in one of the myths that is perpetuated in the English education system – that of the worship of academic intelligence as the supreme aim in life. People can be obsessed by 'intelligence' as *the* way in which to segregate people and even to define their worth.

This is very silly. For a start there are a great many different kinds of intelligence – 'practical', 'emotional', 'creative' and 'verbal' are just four of them, and we all have varying mixtures of these as well as 'academic' intelligence. For another thing, it can be very dangerous when parents and schools focus so much on academic intelligence that many children will feel they have failed – often with tragic consequences.

So we need to work towards taking some responsibility for our failures. Failure is just an inevitable part of life. If we can learn not just to blame others, the life we see out there beyond the wall might not seem so difficult. Taking appropriate responsibility for all aspects of our lives can be very empowering – it can give us the strength to shift several stones.

■ Moving beyond our failures

False guilt and this feeling of being a failure is stuff that belongs in the bin. It is us believing those lies we were told.

It is all too easy to tell ourselves that we are a 'born loser'. But that is total rubbish. No one was born to lose. We were born into an imperfect world with human beings for parents and teachers and when they made a mess of it, we got hurt and our thinking processes got all screwed up. For example, my mother told me repeatedly that I would 'never come to anything'. And I believed her! (You do tend to believe your parents when you are a child.)

So, for me, the failure I experience now (there is rather a lot of it) can get out of proportion. I see it as proof that my mother is right and I am a totally useless person. I still can react this way to failure. I am finding it hard-going to change how I think. I tell myself that deep down I know I am a hopeless and useless person. But I know I must try to change from that brainwashed way of thinking, because otherwise I am perpetuating the lie. And that would let the Monster Mother win – and we cannot have that!

To protect ourselves from failing, we sit behind our wall, realizing that if we risk going out there, failure will inevitably be part of the story. Much easier to sit here. But won't everyone fail at some stage at something? No one gets it right all the time.

Positive Pointer

Every time we fail, or when we face a problem, we can choose to see it as an opportunity to learn something new about ourselves that will make us stronger to face life beyond the wall.

This is an activity that I use often, although now I don't actually draw a chart. This activity can teach us that life out there beyond the wall isn't nearly as bad as we sometimes think it is, and it is effective in helping us to overcome our fear.

Make out a chart like this with three columns and use it to reflect on going out to do things we don't think we want to, for example going to work, to parties, etc., and how much you want to do it.

What lies ahead of me?	How much do I want to go to the party?	How much did I actually enjoy it? (i.e. fill this in after the event)
(e.g. going out to the party)	(e.g. 10%)	(e.g. 90%)

If you are like me, you will often find that something you dread and don't want to do isn't nearly as bad as you expect. Gradually I have learnt from this that what I fear, what I think I will fail at, and what I don't want to have to face, is all part of my negative 'old tapes' and in fact I can get out there and do it. Mostly!

16
Feeling Insignificant in the Universe

It was you who created my inmost self,
  And put me together in my mother's womb.
You know me through and through,
  From having watched my bones take shape
  When I was being formed in secret.

The psalmist, adapted from Psalm 139

I have just watched David Attenborough, on a video about the Antarctic, walking across a part of the polar ice cap. He muses about the vastness of it all and as he walks he says that in the light of this huge solitary stretch of the earth, he as a human being feels insignificant.

Yes. If we have a low view of ourselves, we know that feeling. Then he goes on to say that it is not just that human life seems insignificant, but that it seems irrelevant. I listened to him, stunned at my reaction. I know that feeling of irrelevance. Total uselessness. No purpose. But I found myself objecting to what he said.

■ Human life irrelevant?

How can human life be irrelevant when I know that I feel deep love? When I hug my family and feel the care they give to me? When my mind is marvelling at the complexity of creation as I watch the video and see the seal pup born? That is so beautiful it makes me cry.

Yes, I know the feeling of irrelevance, and although that makes some kind of sense set within the context of the gigantic proportions of earth and space, I also feel my significance to the Great Creator. That he or she cares for me, although I am just a tiny speck within the universe, is the very fact that makes me certain of my value. Years ago, when I could not accept that, I just wanted to be dead because not to feel some significance was so painful that life was torture and I wanted out of it.

The marvels of creation point me to the existence of a Maker and however much I think he or she gets some things in a mess at times, (painful death, wars, the way good people seem to suffer, etc.) I cannot believe that all this wonder and beauty just got here by chance and by some vague process called evolution. To believe it was chance is, to me, a greater step of faith than putting it all down to an artist who enjoyed making beautiful things so much that he made you and me because he wanted to share his love.

■ Chance or creation?

When I see the huge mass of thousands of male emperor penguins, cold and starving as they incubate the newborn chicks, recognizing the voice of their returning mate after their three months at sea, my mind is blown by the wonder of it. He waddles up to her and they dance a greeting before exchanging the chick. She has walked a hundred miles across the ice to get to her baby. He heads off back to sea for his breakfast. Just a hundred miles to get to his first meal for many weeks.

It is the complexity of it that makes me believe that it cannot be chance. It is a bit like what Prince Charles said on the radio on New Year's Day in January 2000. He said that the idea that we human beings are here just by chance is about as likely as a tornado rushing through a car scrapyard producing a complete and fully functioning car!

That I can feel such a sense of amazement at creation, and can feel the beauty warming my inner mind, is for me an aspect of my faith that is precious and important. I can't answer questions about why someone should make a universe and then seem so uncaring about the humans that he (or she) allows some of them to end up in concentration camps or in a mass grave of people who have died of starvation.

I do not have answers. I just have a sense of purpose and significance when I look at the natural world and know that, like the tiny penguin chick, I have a place in the universe and I am watched over and loved. Many chicks are dead before they grow out of grey fluffy feathers. My life may be thrown into chaos tomorrow by the death of my partner or children. I would rage at God. But that would not change my value – even if I found that I turned my back on God because of the suffering. I would still have a place within the plan of it all.

■ Significance and size

Maybe a part of the problem that David Attenborough shows is that he seems to see himself as insignificant because compared with the vastness of it all he is so small. That really is a misunderstanding. Bigness is not in itself a reason for significance.

I know some people judge a person as more worthy or important if they have a big car, but personally I don't buy into that one and we can help ourselves to see some aspects of life if we think that one through. We don't think of viruses and disease-carrying bacteria as insignificant just because they are microscopic, do we? They can defeat the most able of doctors that are millions of times their size.

David Attenborough's feeling of insignificance is a misunderstanding about size and value. As we contemplate our place in this universe, it is that pull towards a Creator who cares about each one of us that I find so compelling and beautiful.

■ A loving hand behind it all

It is interesting how many people I know who, in their younger days, would have nothing to do with God. As they age, they mellow and begin to see some sense in the thought that we are made by an artist who loves what he created. They begin to believe that the whole of life is not some totally irrelevant accident caused by the chance meeting of certain atoms. That there is a loving hand behind it all begins to make more sense.

For some of my friends it was the moment of holding their new baby and experiencing such intense and overwhelming love that helped them to see that there just has to be more than chance governing our lives. For others it was other experiences of love, or just that growing sense of seeing some purpose in it all.

For others, it is when they hit a big crisis in their life that they turn to prayer. They are doing what is natural and appropriate for human beings – they are turning in their need to the Great Creator.

■ Uniquely loved and valued

It is the fact of our creation by a loving Creator which is the thing that gives us value. The Creator cares for us because he made us, just in the way that we care for our family and friends if we are lucky enough to have them. That love and belonging is the basis of our significance. We might be tiny in comparison to the universe, but we are uniquely valued and loved. Just as the penguins put themselves through agony for their babies, so I believe that our Creator does for us. Nothing is too much trouble for the hand that moulded us.

This is me saying this on a good day! Quite a lot of the time it doesn't feel like that! And I often don't behave as if that was what I really believe deep down. That is why I often meditate on the Creator holding and cherishing me in vast hands.

> **Underneath are the everlasting arms.**
>
> Moses, to the people of Israel

I feel loved, valued and of enormous significance and relevance, and a part of my picture of God is a mother penguin who would walk a hundred miles across the ice to get to me.

■ Why can't we see our value and significance?

If we are to start to get out there beyond the wall, we need to work on the whole idea that we have value and significance.

It seems to me that if we have had parents who would trek a hundred miles to get to us when we were little and we needed them, we might understand our own value.

But if they just left us to cry and went out and left us at night with no adult to care for us, or did other things that confused and frightened us, we would have nothing on which we could base thoughts of our own worth. We would instead think:

■ Going to the pub or out to the dance is more important than me.

■ It is not four hours since I was last fed so I am not allowed to need anything yet.

■ There is no time to read me a story because it is time for mum's daily soap on the TV.

■ There are no hugs because in our family no one hugs anyone. (This is easily interpreted by a child who sees other children at school being hugged that she is not worth hugging.)

Positive Pointers

There is love out there.

We are of huge value to the Great Creator.

Activity

Put up some pictures of things you think are beautiful or that fill you with wonder and awe. Treat yourself to a picture calendar each year that does the same thing. If you can't stick things on the wall, make a scrapbook to look through when you want to meditate on beauty.

17
Building Up Our Energy Reserves

I always travel with a fistful of cassettes and CDs and some book of meditation – the *Oxford Book of Prayer* is a wonderful anthology and leaves the mind open and illuminated. It is all too easy in this business [acting] to get to the point where you are just contemplating your navel.

Patricia Routledge, actress, talking about how she survives
the rigours of filming and being away from home

If we are now ready to consider going out there beyond our wall for extended amounts of time, we need to be sure that we have a place to return to where we can feel safe and protected and can build up our energy reserves again. How we build up those energy reserves will vary according to the things we enjoy as individuals.

I have a very special box in my safe place (my bedroom) and I keep in it things that have a special meaning for me. I covered a box in my favourite fabric and on good days I try to think of things that help me to feel good, such as a photo with good memories, or a special letter or card. I put these special things in my box as a kind of 'safety net' for days that are a struggle. Then I can retreat to my room where I can be alone and I look through my box and remind myself of the good things. This helps to lift my mood and I try to remind myself that I am not a bad and worthless person, I have value and the bad time will pass.

I have shared the idea of a special box with many people now and it is exciting to hear people saying that once they finally got around to making the box, they found it hugely encouraging and helpful.

It tells us:

■ **We value ourselves.**

■ **We love ourselves.**

■ **We are worth taking trouble over. We are valuable, and special people.**

■ Being kind to ourselves

Making a space where we can build ourselves up is an example of valuing ourselves enough to give time to something that can make us feel good. It is about being kind to ourselves. It helps us to build up those good feelings and lets them become more dominant in our thinking and feeling patterns so that eventually those more positive things we tell ourselves begin to replace all those negative messages we received in the past.

As well as my special box by my bed, I have created a little thinking space in my room with a special cushion to sit on, and a shelf that has a wooden cross, a candle, photos of my children and wonderful partner, some special rocks and fossils, favourite pictures including puffins and penguins, a favourite shell, a picture a child in my class drew for me which says, 'Jesus is the light of the dark,' a picture of a little child held safe in the hands of God, a folder of letters people wrote to me about my book on depression, a poem written for me by my daughter and a row of books – a Bible, books of poems and prayers.

I found that I had so many special pictures and cards that I started putting them in a scrapbook along with some photos and I am seeing this as a way of remaking my life. Like most of the people I talked to who experience low self-esteem, I had a difficult start in life and as I make this scrapbook, it feels like I am redeeming my childhood.

That feels good.

So what I have done is I have made a space in my life where I can sit and meditate, feel safe, build up my confidence to go out there again, and where I know that I've tried hard to value myself.

■ Redeeming our childhood

> **The surest cure for the feeling of being an unacceptable person is the discovery that we are accepted by the grace of One whose acceptance of us matters most...**
> **To experience grace is to recover our lost inner child...**
> **Shame cheats us of childhood. Grace gives it back to us.**
> Lewis Smedes, *Shame and Grace*, p. 108

I am finding it helpful to turn the painful memories of childhood into something more positive in various ways.

■ **Buying back the special books I loved so much by seeking them out in second-hand bookshops. They make good reading for times when a children's book is just right.**

■ **Looking through old photos and reliving some of the events and, as I do this, reassuring my 'lost inner child' that it was tough, that adults did terrible things, and it is OK to feel upset. It is as I listen to that frightened child that I find my feelings are becoming less overwhelming. Phobias are gradually disappearing.**

■ **I use my teddies and other 'creatures' to talk about the trust I lost as a child.**

This betrayal of trust is the nub of our lost self-esteem in childhood. It is loss of trust and our overwhelming fear that we will be abandoned that sent us behind the wall in the first place.

Positive Pointers

Practise trusting people. However much we have been let down in the past, we are never going to get out from behind the wall unless we take a risk and trust people.

When we do something well we must resist saying, 'That was actually no big deal.' (I am so good at that!) Yes, it is a big deal!

You did it! Freeze everything. Stop for a moment and tell yourself you did it well.

Activity

Take time to find a box and seek out pictures, etc., that make you feel good, such as snow-capped mountains. Try to think of the box as a 'safety net' for the really bad times.

Remind yourself that you are taking time to put together the box because you are 'worth it'.

Part 5

Making a Hole Big Enough to Creep Out

18
Who Am I?

A journey of a thousand miles begins with a single step.

Chinese proverb

Hopefully a time will come when we decide that we will make a hole big enough in our wall to creep out into the world beyond quite frequently. This puts more demands on us to change how we think, to change some of our attitudes and to develop a 'can do' attitude to living out there beyond the wall.

I was struck by how many of the older people whom I talked to, or who wrote to me, mentioned trying to find out what makes themselves 'tick'. I suppose we tend to think of finding out 'who we are' as a young person's task, but in mid-life we can encounter things that make us re-evaluate our lives and rethink what we want to do and the person we want to be.

It is noticeable how many women go through this rethinking as their children get older and they start to plan their post-children career. Working in teacher training, it was alarming to see the number of marriage problems that arose as (mostly) women came to train for a new career.

The degree made demands on them which required partners to take a share in child care and domestic tasks. Then the problems would start to surface. The old patterns of their life needed to be reassessed and I saw that when this happens, there is a need for change, and where change is happening, there will almost inevitably be conflict.

■ Reassessing our lives

This process of change is, I think, what can happen in anyone's life, and often that conflict will be within ourselves and that is tough going. If we also have low self-esteem, 'life events' and other times of change can be very influential.

Big things (such as relationships breaking up and the death of someone we love) happen to us and these can be terribly difficult to face. The change and conflict we might be thrown into can be life-changing.

■ Why did I react that way?

We find ourselves wondering quite why we reacted to a situation in a particular way.

- ■ Why did that matter so much to me?
- ■ Why am I getting these panic attacks?
- ■ Why did I behave that way in that particular group?
- ■ Why do I so desperately not want to go to that party?

One of the things that happens as we go on in life (and particularly in therapy) is that we find out much more about ourselves. The person we thought we knew fairly well at 20, seems to be much more complex and mysterious at 30.

For me, one of the most unexpected things was to discover how powerful some understanding of 'the child within' can be. When the whole idea of that was first put to me, I thought it completely crazy. Set within the whole notion of ourselves as having several different 'people' as part of our personality, I could see the locked doors of the mental hospital looming and I could not cope with the whole idea.

Gradually, though, I came to see that I am made up of lots of different 'people', one of whom is a very hurt and confused little girl, and it is as I have come to understand these different 'people' inside me that I seem to feel better about myself.

As well as my beloved teddy, I have a whole family of 'creatures' who are different bits of myself and help me to cope with life beyond the wall. I found a wonderful little doll one day and completely fell in love with her and bought her. This might sound totally crazy, but by talking to her, I have found considerable healing. Our inner child is important.

> **When you experience joy, sadness, anger, fear, or affection your Child Within is coming out. When you are truly feeling your feelings you are allowing your Inner Child to be. Your Child Within is also active when you are being playful, spontaneous, creative, intuitive, and surrendering to the spiritual self. The experience of these states is often referred to as 'being in your Inner Child'. When you share this state with others it is referred to as 'coming from your Inner Child.'**
>
> Lucia Capacchione, *Recovery of Your Inner Child*

■ What kind of person am I?

As well as having been hugely influenced by our past life, some psychologists work on the whole idea of different personality types. This is very interesting and has helped many people to understand themselves better.

So we can come to see ourselves as either 'introverted' or 'extroverted' and sometimes a mixture of both, depending on the circumstances. We might be someone who relies a great deal on intuition – or we might hate people who do that.

Understanding ourselves in terms of how we prefer to think and be in our life can give us insight into who we are, and for me, it gave me some grounds for starting to accept myself as I am. Once I could see that I so much prefer to be on my own because this is just how I am, I began to be less negative towards myself. I had thought my wish to hide away behind my brick wall because I cannot manage life was something I should be able to overcome. I was, I told myself, just being pathetic. So learning to see that introverts are just like that has helped me to be less self-critical.

For other people, the highlight of the week is going out

with friends. This is how they feel good about themselves and how they recharge their batteries. After a party they feel great and can face life again. For me, having to go out and lecture or go to a meeting or whatever is terribly demanding. I come home exhausted, often tearful, and need plenty of time on my own at home to recover.

Of course, the whole thing about personality types is much more complex than just about introverts or extroverts and if you want to read more, there are some books listed in the Resources section at the end of the book.

Some people with whom I work professionally find it hard to see me as an introvert. What we see of people in public is what they choose to show us, and that may only be a very tiny part of that person. None of us can make assumptions about others simply based on outward signs!

■ Understanding ourselves

We are all complex mixtures of past influences, personality, our own aims and ambitions, our different ways of behaving in different groups and so on, and the process of understanding ourselves is probably ongoing through all our life. For me, the process is helped by having a journal to record my growing understandings of myself, recording what I cannot understand or want to work on. But journal writing for me goes in phases. If it doesn't grab you to write, try having a 'thinking time' two or three times a week when you can put on some music and sit and meditate, maybe focusing on a flower, or a beautiful stone, or you could light a candle.

Positive Pointers

Look for the very best in people.

Seek, and speak, the truth.

Nurture your 'inner child'.

Try to answer some of these questions. It is probably best to write down what you think and date it, leaving plenty of space on the page to come back to it in a year and compare it with how you feel then.

1. Am I mostly an introvert and get my energy from being on my own, or do I prefer to be with people?

2. Or am I a mixture?

3. How do I tend to react in a group? (e.g. are you a good leader?)

4. What kind of person am I at work?

5. What kind of person am I when I am with my family?

6. What do I need to do to feel good about myself?

7. What treat can I give myself for working hard at all this self-esteem stuff?

8. What can I do to get closer to my long-term goals today?

19
How Do I Know That I Have Value?

Changing your self-esteem can only come about through another kind of relationship which is an intense, enduring, loving, accepting and affirming relationship with yourself.

Tony Humphreys

On our short journeys out into the world from behind the wall we become aware that more confident people seem to have a way of valuing themselves.

■ **They take care of themselves.**

■ **They are kind to themselves.**

■ **They say, 'I know I'm worth it' (and not just in the shampoo adverts!).**

It comes through very strongly talking to people with low self-esteem that one of the things they have lost is any sense of their personal value.

■ We are a mixture of good and bad

It is very important that we see ourselves and other people as a mixture of good and bad.

One of the most noticeable things about talking to people with low self-esteem – and I am right there with them – is that we see ourselves as totally bad or useless. Other people we might see as totally good (or that is what we might have thought as a child – 'Mummy must be good because she is Mummy. I must be bad because I upset Mummy').

This black-and-white thinking is rather like the way

adolescents think and we really do need to be a bit more balanced about it. Rather than telling ourselves we are completely hopeless, maybe it is better to identify our 'hopeless' bits and accept we need longer to change (e.g. one person wrote to me, 'I get inside [my parent's house] and I completely fall back into little-girl mode and they bully me just the way they always have').

Alongside those old reactions we were brainwashed into, we can put our new thinking that we have good bits too, and we are working on making those more dominant in our life.

■ But being 'good' or 'bad' is still not about our value

I get horribly mixed up with any value I might give myself being linked to both how 'good' I am, and, as I have said before, I tend unhelpfully to measure my value by what I achieve. Over and over again I found this view was held by people I questioned.

Of course, being able to achieve is great. To have paid work, for example, can contribute towards our feelings of valuing ourselves. Any kind of working can give us feelings of success, achievement and maybe even help us to feel that there is some point to life!

The problem I see in myself and in others who think in the same way is that I tend to value myself *only* through what I do. That is, I think, unhealthy and I have felt this for some years. However, I still find it incredibly difficult to value myself just for who I am. I can only point to things I have done.

It is easier for me to see value in others. So, I sit on the plane listening to the steward telling us what to do if we come down in the sea, and how to get myself out of the plane. She is doing all of that because people have value. (I shut my mind to the reality of what would actually happen if the plane came down in the sea. It is an essential life skill in my view to be able to shut out reality and go along with whatever little fantasy is being played out at the time.)

I understood the worry my family went through when I was away teaching in the Middle East and some missile exchanges went on and people were told to get out of Jerusalem. We were told to get out because the people in the embassy thought we had value – we needed to be safe. My family were worried because they value me.

■ We need to know about our value

I once heard an evangelist on American television say something along the lines that God valued those who worked hard and rewarded them with wealth because of their value, strongly implying that the poor and out of work were lazy and of less value to God!

What utterly stupid and dangerous nonsense!

But it is a lot easier to sit here and type this than believe in my own value. This chapter has been the hardest to write of the whole book so far. I find it so very hard to see that I have any value, although the messages of love from my family are very powerful.

I find that I can sense my value more easily if I think of God and how he or she seems to value me. I can kind of accept that degree of love and care from God. So, I suppose, if really pushed to say how I know that I have value, I would say that I think God values me.

That might seem stupid to you. For all I know it might seem pretty stupid to God. But I reckon that if I sit through therapy twice a week to try to see that I am loved and I have value, then at least if I can attribute loving and caring thoughts to a being I cannot prove exists, it has to be at least somewhere to start.

Our value as human beings is something we get as an all-inclusive package deal from the Great Creator along with life, blood, the ability to breathe and a love of chocolate. Some of us are just very skilled at refusing to believe in that 'given' value and insist that we must in some way earn value and the right to take up space on the planet.

■ Valuing others, valuing ourselves

If you are a person who doesn't beat people up, or steal or break into old people's houses to rob them, you probably value people. Even if we do engage in some anti-social behaviour, if we know we wish we didn't, then we value other people.

But the crunch is, do we value ourselves?

I was on a plane the other day and the man next to me kept sniffing. It drove me crazy. I moaned about it to my friend Alice when I reached my destination. 'Did you value yourself enough to ask the steward if you could move?' she asked. No. I didn't. I sat there, glad that this was only a short flight. But I learnt from that. I need to learn to value myself more and ask for things that I need.

So this week when I was on another flight the man next to me had his newspaper open and his arm took up the whole of the arm rest and was well into what I regarded as my space. I plucked up the courage to ask if I could move – and I did and felt really good about it. I'd valued myself enough to be kind to myself.

The more I think about this chapter and the whole idea of developing our self-esteem, it seems to me that the skill of being kind to ourselves is a key idea in the book.

Positive Pointers

If we change our beliefs and our values we can change our lives.

If we are kind to ourselves, we will like ourselves more.

Activity

If we want to improve our self-esteem, we must have some idea of where we are trying to get to. This is an activity that might take some time. You need to:

1. Write a few words about what 'success' means to you. It might be 'getting promotion', 'finding a partner', 'being a good person that people want to be with', 'being a good parent', 'being at peace with myself', 'getting better from depression', and so on.

2. Write a few words about what you really value in life – those big things that you think make up a good and successful person and which you admire in others and which you try to teach your children, nieces, nephews (and your class if you are a teacher).

My list starts like this:

- positive thinking

- kindness

- honesty

- integrity

- sense of humour

and so on.

3. Now this is the crunch. If that is what you admire in others, these are the things you want for yourself if you are to feel successful. You need to come back to your list often to see if you are working towards making these values part of your own life.

20
Giving and Receiving Affirmation

**Give me the ability to see good things in unexpected
places and talents in unexpected people, and give me,
O Lord, the grace to tell them so.**

From a 17th-century nun's prayer

If I am going to survive outside the wall for longer periods,
I need to feel reasonably safe out there. Part of that sense of
safety can come from feeling affirmed and valued.

■ Feeling OK

The earliest memory that I have of feeling OK about myself is
at junior school when I was about eight. We had a supply
(stand-in) teacher and she had clearly remembered me from a
previous visit of hers. As she went around the class learning our
names, when she came to me she had remembered my name
and she smiled at me and was incredibly positive towards me.
I remember being completely stunned. I had not remembered
her. Out of the whole class she was only like that to me.

I can still remember that feeling. She is being like that to me!
I felt warm and comfortable and the intense pleasure of that
incident is something I can still feel. It is so real I can touch it.

That same feeling was there for a little while in therapy
with John and it is sometimes there as I talk with Ruth. I am
starting to realize that it is there in my relationships with my
family, but it has taken me a long time to recognize it with
them and let myself receive it and let it touch my soul.

■ Giving affirmation

I learnt as a teacher of small children to be very affirming and
positive towards children, their parents and my colleagues.

For example, with a small child who is not yet reading, or a new young teacher who is struggling with her class, I soon learnt that affirmation was the way to get them going. I would start from what they could already do with some confidence, then move on from there.

Then when I started looking at books about self-esteem I found the advice is that if we start being affirming towards others, we find that this itself can help our own self-esteem to develop. That just might be true, so it is worth a go.

■ What about our inner life?

We have probably all met the kind of person who seems to be bitter and angry on the inside, and who is given to criticisms and negative attitudes to those around them, spitting nastiness whenever they can like a bad-tempered camel. (I went to a camel market once at Beersheba, and believe me, camels are bad-tempered and they are champions of the universe at spitting.)

I am not sure what that kind of attitude says about such a person's inner life, but presumably they are not happy, nor would it seem likely that they would help those around them feel good about themselves. It would be reasonable to assume that those people who do camel impersonations don't have a very good sense of their own value, so being a camel is one way they manage life. I hide behind my brick wall to survive, they become camels.

At times I know I get into camel mode and it is something we need to be aware of in ourselves. If we are tired, the children are being noisy, we can't find a parking place to get something urgently from the pharmacy, something has gone wrong at work, we feel depressed, then we get home to find some small thing that annoys us, it is just too easy to spread our inner anger and frustration to those around us.

As I talked with more people about self-esteem and as I thought about my family, friends and acquaintances, it seemed to me that camel people are often hurt people. But the problem is that it is all too easy to pass on that negative attitude to life to those around us, especially children. Then, if we give out negative vibes, people are unlikely to feed us back positive ones, so it all escalates, from a hurt individual, to a negative-thinking group of people who feel bad about themselves.

One way out of this cycle of negative attitude and low self-esteem seems to be to affirm others and to let ourselves receive affirmation.

■ Accepting compliments

Years ago I discovered that I am no good at accepting compliments and I think that was one of the first things I saw as an example of my low self-esteem. I was holding my toddler son in my arms and said to one of the psychiatric nurses in the hospital, 'Isn't he beautiful?', and he replied, 'Just like his mum.' I hit the roof. I was furious. I felt tearful. I could hardly contain my feelings. My world went into chaos.

Of course, that was picked up by the nurse and I had several very uncomfortable conversations about it over the next few weeks, and ended up learning a great deal – though it took me many years to get a grip on the main issue – that I was believing my mother's view of me that I was ugly, stupid and useless.

What I try to do now is say 'thank you' if people compliment me, and not brush it off. That's tough, so that's part of the activity for this chapter.

■ Believing we can change

One of the reasons why I wanted to write this book is that I know that I have changed and so I believe that it is possible for everyone to change. I know I keep saying this, but it really is very important.

OK, we may never get ourselves to the 'Give me a long enough lever and I'll move the world' kind of mentality, but we can make small changes in ourselves which, if we keep working at them, can significantly change our lives (and the lives of those around us) for the better. If a little voice inside you is saying that it might be all very well for that Sue to be able to change, but you are a special case and will never be able to change, then that little voice is part of your past life and you need to tell it, firmly but kindly, to shut up.

This is where you need a rainbow book. Write some of your reactions to this chapter in the margin, or your journal, then put the book by your bed where you can come back to it again and again over months and years.

Positive Pointers

We *can* change our inner lives by affirming others and by letting ourselves receive good things about ourselves.

Making positive steps to reduce our stress can significantly change the quality of our life.

Activity

1. Try to be affirming to those around you. Make a plan to say at least one affirming thing to one person every day for a week.

2. Your affirming might also include giving compliments, but you might be able to do that separately. Again, plan to give a compliment every day for a week.

3. (Much harder than 1 and 2!) Work at being able to say 'thank you' when you are complimented. It is hard, but try not to cast the compliment aside as this can upset people. If all you can manage is a smile as you blush, that is still progress.

21
Love, Value and Death

O joy that seekest me through pain,
 I cannot close my heart to thee:
I trace the rainbow through the rain,
 And feel the promise is not vain,
 That morn shall tearless be.

From a hymn by George Matheson (d. 1906)

The only thing we can be certain of in life is that we will all die. We will all have to face 'life events' that are so big and important to us that we are forced to think in depth about what love is and what we really value in life. These are times when we have an opportunity to change our views of ourselves and our self-esteem.

My dog Jemma died at 3.30 this morning. She died in my arms. I lay beside her on the bed realizing that my world was about to be changed for ever. I told her how much I love her. How for all of us she was so special and so loved that to be without her will make our lives totally different. I couldn't bear the thought that she might be suffering. Her body had clearly given up. She had gone floppy and her breathing had changed. I knew she was dying so I asked God to take her quickly. If he ever loved me at all to take her now. Then she just stopped breathing. Her little body made one twitch and I held her, fearful that she would feel pain and confusion, but she lay quite still.

I wake my daughter and we lie on the bed beside the lifeless body. We don't believe she can be dead and we look for signs of life. We wish we had done things differently. If only we had done something else maybe she would still be alive. We feel guilt, pain, anger and a kind of emptiness and shock. Life for us will never be quite the same again.

■ Love stays for ever

My daughter tells me her friend's theory that when you love someone and they are part of your life, there is a little bit of your heart that is them and when they die, a bit of them is left behind in you and you will never be the same again. Our lives are changed for ever by knowing that person. That is what it feels like. Knowing Jemma was like knowing a person, but her love was so steadfast, so ongoing, so uncomplicated by anything that it has kept me sane through almost 10 years of what has been a very difficult phase of life. My life is changed for the better by knowing her.

I wish I had spent much longer last night rubbing her tummy. She loved that. She would lie on her back and grin and let you rub her for as long as you had the patience to do it. I know that when we lose someone we love we always feel some guilt, but my guilt over this lack of time spent with her feels too real just to be the kind of emotion so common at death.

Things will be very different now. There will be no little face that peers through the cat flap as I return home and unlock the door. She would wag her tail and bounce up and down, so pleased to see me. She made coming home so joyous. Even if I had just gone to post a letter she greeted me like I had just been away for a month.

■ Unconditional love

I wonder how I will cope with the death of my partner or children if I am like this when my dog dies. Maybe any kind of death is so hard that each one has its own kind of pain and its own particular devastations. I am finding it hard knowing that when my mother dies, I think I will feel less pain than I feel now at losing Jemma. I am sure of Jemma's love and devotion to me. My mother gives few clues to any kinds of feelings of affection for me.

I will wish it could have been different with my mother too. I expect guilt will feature in my feelings, but I have spent my adult life working on not feeling that guilt at her death because it would not be real guilt. I think when she dies I will also feel great relief.

I spend hours trying to come to terms with Jemma's death. When I say how much it hurts, my partner says that he thinks this is the price we pay when we love someone that much. I think of this as an equal and opposite force. The more you love someone, the greater will the pain be when they die. I know that if I had to go through this pain because I loved Jemma that much then I will bear the pain willingly for her. I would not have wanted to love her any less so that my pain would be less.

With Jemma I felt good about myself. She made me feel important. I mattered to her. She made me feel I had value. What I said and did mattered.

There is a lesson here about the people we mix with. It doesn't do our self-esteem any good to be with those who moan about life. That just drags us down. We need to be with those who are positive and who are striving to make their life, and the lives of those around them, full of the kind of love that brings joy, peace and contentment, whatever their physical circumstances.

I have a picture of Jemma now in my mind. She is in a large field and there is long, lush, green grass and a stream at the edge of the field with the most beautiful fresh and clear running water. No more London tap water for her. In the background are snow-capped mountains and as the moon appears and the evening star starts to show, she settles down to sleep on a bed of dried grass. Life for her now will not be lampposts and busy roads but chasing spiders through the undergrowth and running in the freedom of the field.

Death is the only certain thing about life and if we can creep out from behind the wall sometimes, we need to face up to the inevitability that death will happen to those we love (and those we hate). Guilt and many other huge feelings will inevitably arise within us.

I have never felt so profoundly that all that is good and lovely and joyous comes from God. He let us borrow Jemma for a few short years but now he wants her back. I feel such gratitude for those years. It has included times when life felt far too threatening and the world such a frightening place. But Jemma made parts of it less of a struggle. I'll never forget such unconditional love, her happy grin and her great gift of being just plain silly.

Positive Pointers

Surrounded by positive people, we can grow beyond our low self-esteem.

Surrounded by unconditional love, we too can learn to love.

Activity

What do we really want in life? So many people seem to be:

■ living where they don't really want to live.

■ living their lives in a way that doesn't really satisfy them.

■ doing the kinds of work that they don't want to do. (If you are an artist, I am not saying, 'Give up your day job'. We all have to live and if you want to be an actor or whatever, that boring job is a part of that kind of life.)

If we want to change aspects of our life we do need to recognize that some things cannot be changed, but lots can if we are determined enough about it.

1. Write a list of what you really want out of life. Brainstorm it quickly on a bit of paper, then add to it over the next few days.

2. Think through what you would need to change to start to lead the kind of life you really want.

3. The small things can be easier to change – and we can change them. Every one of us can make a decision to change aspects of our life.

Things you think about might include some of these decisions.

■ **Watch less TV and take up a hobby or go to an evening class.**

■ **Decide to go for a brisk walk every morning before breakfast.**

■ **Talk with a partner about changing some aspect of your domestic life.**

4. Don't be frightened of the big things! If you want to move out of the city and get a cottage in the country, or whatever, you will never do it unless you decide just to go for it. I thoroughly recommend resigning from a job that has just got too stressful or whatever. You do need to think through financial implications, but doing it is one of the best feelings ever.

22
Forgiving is Letting Go

Carrying around a burden of hatred for someone is a very heavy thing to bear for the person who is doing the hating. The person who is hated probably does not know anything about it. When I forgave [my Japanese prisoner of war guard] a great weight went from me, and I felt such relief. If we cling onto old hatreds, we damage ourselves. We must let them go and move on.

An American soldier talking about his
experiences in a Japanese prison

If our self-esteem is low because of something someone did to us, then some kind of forgiveness is probably needed if we are to avoid becoming bitter. Bitterness and unresolved anger towards another human being is so uncreative and potentially explosive. I know from my own experiences how bitterness can poison even the loveliest of people, turning them from being a source of love and positive growth for those around them to a source of unhappiness and pain.

■ We want justice

None of us escapes from the likelihood of becoming bitter. The minute we see that if what was done to us should not have been done to us, we have the human tendency to want some kind of compensation. They wronged us and owe us something. Justice needs to be done. Revenge seems a good idea. Or cutting ourselves off from them for a while – or for ever.

We, rightly, feel angry, but it is not always possible to say to someone, 'You wronged me and I'm angry with you.'

■ You might not be assertive enough to say it.

■ You might know if you said it, more chaos and hurt would be the result.

■ The person may be dead.

■ The 'person' that wronged you may not be one person at all, but a whole 'system' – the health service, or the council office who you think should find you a home, or the firm that made you redundant.

We are often powerless to try to get what we see as justice.

I have noticed that after traumatic accidents, we see people on the news who want justice (which sometimes means revenge) for the loss of a loved one. If an aeroplane fell out of the sky, or a boat was run down by another bigger boat, or some idiot was found to have been drinking and driving, we rightly want and expect – and deserve – justice. But if the inquiry set up doesn't have the outcome we think it should, or the government won't set up the inquiry, or the police behaved like morons or whatever, we feel not just bereaved, but we feel we owe it to the lost loved one to fight for justice (though we might mean retribution) so that the same thing cannot happen again.

■ Stopping the bitterness growing

What I have said so far is all very rational. But over and over again, we see on the news, or know personally, people who go on and on fighting for what they see as justice, while the bitterness inside them grows. They show clearly that they are unable and unwilling to 'let it go'. It takes over their life. The obsession grows.

I know that if a child of mine were killed in an accident that was caused by negligence, I too would want justice. I would not want anyone else to suffer like that. To lose a child would be for me the most painful thing that I could possibly imagine.

■ A fight for justice

I would fight to the end for justice for my child, but when I see people screwed up and almost taken over by obsession striving for what they see as justice, I wonder if there isn't something else needed here.

A wrong deserves some kind of justice. Of course that is right. A fight to prevent some terrible disaster from happening again is of course right. But I truly believe that another thing is coming into play here, and that is the mental and spiritual well-being of ourselves and those around us. I believe that we have to let go. To stop demanding justice. To give up our quest for retribution.

■ Forgive and forget?

I am not talking about 'forgive and forget'. I don't believe in that. My friend's husband has just walked out on her after 30 years of marriage. He 'fell in love' with someone else and just walked out. She is not likely to forget that, nor are her children. But she wrote me a letter in which I can see that, just a few weeks after the event, she is already beginning to forgive. She is not going to forget what he did. Never.

But she is already on the road

- **■ to forgiving him.**

- **■ to starting again.**

- **■ to getting beyond it.**

- **■ to telling herself that she has to get on with her life, although she feels devastated and hardly knows how to get through a day.**

She and the children are so desperately hurt, but they are not letting it turn to bitterness inside themselves. Already she is expressing the thought that in some way good will come out of it all. That is an amazing thing to be able to do at this stage.

Forgive and forget is another one of those things that we are told we 'ought' to do. But forgetting huge wrongs, or painful events we experience, is impossible!

We may even be told that if we don't 'forget' God will not forgive us! What total and utter junk that is.

I think it is crucial to our future well-being that we accept there are some things we will never forget *and that is not wrong*.

■ Letting go

What I think is the human way to deal with those abusive, cruel, or even just teasing things that were done is to set a goal of letting those things go – growing beyond them and getting on with living our lives free from bitterness. We can call this forgiving.

We can forgive even though we remember. That is realistic.

Eventually we may get the inner strength even to find that we start to wish the person well who wronged us. But that might not happen for a long time and that does not matter.

Forgiveness is hard. I am actually not that skilled at it! I don't quite know if I am 'meant' to feel it inside. Or do I just know I am 'letting it go' in my head and intending to forgive? Or is it a mixture of all those things? I don't know.

What I do know is that when I do find the strength to forgive it is more for my benefit than for the wrongdoer. It is my inner self that could be damaged if I cling onto old hates and bitterness. By 'letting go' I have a fresh start and can gradually feel free of my anger.

■ Forgiving ourselves

The real crunch is can we forgive ourselves? Or do we persist at 'beating ourselves up'?

Checking through some artist's roughs of a book last week, I was apologizing to the desk editor that I can't have explained something well enough for the artists. 'Stop beating yourself up, Sue,' she said. 'Your explanation was perfectly good, so stop apologizing. You are far too hard on yourself.'

I realized I knew she was right. I didn't have to take all the responsibility for things not being perfect first time around.

■ We can be so busy 'beating ourselves up' that we are failing to see that, like everybody else, we run best on affirmation and forgiveness.

■ Forgiving ourselves is a hard but necessary process.

■ We need to acknowledge that, like everyone else, we sometimes get, and do, things wrong.

■ As we learn to let those things go, we can accept ourselves as we are. Weak, frail people sometimes, but whatever it is that we might have done for which we feel we need forgiveness, we can get beyond it.

■ We must not let guilt for anything that we might have *done* turn into shame for *who we are* as people. The two things are quite different – and we need to keep telling ourselves that over and over again. It's a hard concept to grasp if we have spent most of our life feeling both guilt and shame and muddling them up.

Positive Pointers

Forgiving someone can set you free.

Forgiving is the surest way to free yourself of bitterness.

Activity

Forgiveness is a complex mixture of thoughts, feelings and actions so it needs working at. Sometimes it might be that any forgiveness will take years to achieve because it is more of a long-term thinking process than an event that we can give a date.

1. You need to work out who wronged you and what you think was wrong. This can be hard if the wrong was part of your early childhood when you don't really know exactly what happened. Childhood abuse comes into this category.

2. Then you can try to think through what the wrong has meant for you. People I talked to were angry at people and systems who had 'ruined' their life. It can be all too easy to pretend that anger isn't there, yet it is very scary to admit that it is. Ideally, talk to someone about this. A self-help group might be a good place to start to 'let go'.

If you are really struggling with forgiving someone, you might find Lewis Smedes book *Forgive and Forget* very helpful to work through. For me, it was one of my most positive 'life events' to work through this book slowly applying Lewis Smedes' wisdom to myself.

23
Learning to Laugh

During moments of laughter we experience what it is to be connected, unified and perfectly integrated – there are no barriers and no falsities. Laughter is soulful.

Robert Holden, *Laughter: The Best Medicine*

However much I feel down, I can almost always see the funny side of something. This gets the interesting reaction from some that I cannot possibly be feeling down if I can laugh and make jokes – but, of course, your sense of humour doesn't necessarily leave you when depression grips you.

When I began to think about this, I realized that humour could be one way to try to defeat both our depression and our low self-esteem. There seems to be some evidence of this. I read somewhere that laughing relaxes you, and that does seem to be true. So I have tried out humour as a way of lifting my mood and it really does work.

If I am deeply depressed, it can be a major task just to get myself to go downstairs, make a cup of tea and put the television on. (I usually can't read when I am very depressed, so opening a Bill Bryson book – a great way to find myself laughing out loud – is for better days.)

I play favourite videos and I have found that just by doing that simple thing, I can start to feel better. I watch *Independence Day* and enter into the fantasy, or I watch Bruce Willis or Harrison Ford save the world. After that, having to come out from behind my brick wall and cope with the world doesn't seem quite so bad.

■ Laughing

Playing funny videos is an extension of this sense I have that all is well with the world providing I don't think about it too much. So it is fine to go into some fantasy because that helps me not to dwell on the reality of life.

I felt deeply understood by my daughter last week on Christmas Day when she gave me the complete set of Fawlty Towers videos. Seeing that my daughter understood how much laughter means to me was itself something that made me smile.

Laughing makes me feel better. It is as simple as that. I watch Basil shake his fists at God, make blunder after blunder, getting himself increasingly deeper and deeper into his lies, and somehow it is easier to think that life could go on.

John Cleese (as Basil) is so funny because he is so unbelievably dreadful when faced with a crisis. It is utterly excruciating to watch, but that is what is so delicious about it. I might be making a total mess of my life, but Basil is making a worse job and I think laughing at another person's fictitious misfortunes with life and feeling our toes curl in embarrassment is very releasing.

Life is so complex and confusing that laughing at it seems to help.

■ Escapism

I suppose that some people could brush all this off and say it is 'escapism'. Yes, I agree. That is exactly what it is. Wonderful, wonderful escapism that helps me for a while to get out of the terrible reality of a world I cannot quite cope with into one that is far less demanding.

Really funny moments are partly so amusing because we recognize something of our embarrassed humanness within them. Recognizing and learning to live with our human vulnerability seems to me to be an essential life skill. Like many people, I go to pieces if I think someone is laughing at me, but if someone will laugh with me, that is completely different. Life beyond the wall becomes a bit less scary for a moment.

Positive Pointers

Laugh a lot.

Smile a lot, even when you are on your own.

Activity

1. Think carefully about what it is that makes you laugh. It might be going out to the pub with some friends, or listening to a funny show on the radio or television, or reading particular books. Write some sentences that start: 'I laugh when...'

2. Think through and make a plan to have these things available when you feel really bad about yourself and unable to face the world. You could put some things in your special box (see Chapter 17), or build up a set of funny books or videos, or plan to see a friend who always makes you feel better.

24
Poor Me

They can do all because they think they can.

Virgil

Self-pity is about as attractive as that unbelievably smelly mud you get in salt marshes that my dog Jemma used to run through. I see it in some people I know. I see it in myself. It is terrible stuff that clings to us like a bad smell. If we are to live successfully out there beyond the wall, we need to get rid of this self-pity, or others will not want to be near us.

Of course we can be realistic about our lives. We need to be able to look back at things that happened and be quite honest and say, 'That was hell'. A part of our brick wall protection system can be that we say, 'That's fine that happened and I don't feel angry or upset.' (Psychologists call this denial.)

We need to acknowledge the terribleness of it. This is crucial for our future mental health. But it is equally crucial not to let self-pity engulf us. It can become like stinking, sinking mud and it will make us stink and at its worst it could suck us down so that we disappear.

■ Letting ourselves feel the pain

I have my notes for this chapter beside me. I am typing away quite happily with my teddy beside me and my morning cup of tea, but a feeling of unease is taking over. Here I am writing about being honest about the awfulness of life and letting ourselves feel how bad it was. Yet that is the very thing I cannot do. It is one of the most dominant features of my work with Ruth and when I see her next, almost inevitably my refusal to let myself acknowledge and feel my deepest real feelings will be part of what we talk about.

So, here I am feeling a complete fraud, typing this stuff about being real and honest about what has happened to us, when all the time that is something I am just completely hopeless at doing. (Whoops! Those negative 'old tapes' are going again.)

■ It isn't the scale of the badness

It is not just what is done to us, but our interpretation and our reaction to what was done and the effect that it has on our life, especially our inner life, that is so bad.

So, some people not only have low self-esteem because of some 'bad' things happening to them, but this is compounded because they trivialize the events, brush them off, and then feel even worse because they say they have so little reason to feel bad about themselves, so they feel even worse.

It isn't the scale of the badness. It is what sense we made of it at the time, and the meaning that it has for us now. If we were sexually abused as a child we might still feel those hurts in the ways in which we felt them as a child. We still want to retreat to the corner with our teddy and our comfort blanket.

> **When we don't acknowledge our pain, it will be transferred into a bodily symptom, anger or something equally destructive. Saying yes means letting in the pain full force, knowing you will not only get to the other side of it, but also gain something in the end – if you look for it.**
>
> Susan Jeffers

For me, the verbal abuse I received as a child could seem trivial. But it has so affected my life that I can see that it is not really trivial. I was taught as child to say, 'Sticks and stones will break my bones, but names will never hurt me.' That is utter rubbish. I am deeply hurt by the things my mother, stepfather and brothers said to me.

Stan, one of the people who wrote to me about self-esteem, had his life wrecked by teachers not seeing his real problem –

dyslexia. So he did not get the help he needed and this has resulted in him having poor qualifications. No one committed a criminal offence. But lack of thought and care means his quality of life is poor and it is hard to see how it could change.

But, whatever was done to us, however 'big' or 'small' we regard those events, self-pity is just as ugly. It is us behaving as 'victims'. We became victims as defenceless children, but we must stop behaving as victims now.

We have to find ways to get out of the habit of feeling so sorry for ourselves, for it will only drag us further down, making us unpleasant to be with, and this will, in turn, contribute to our feelings that we need to hide behind our brick wall.

Positive Pointers

Keep developing the 'can do' attitude to life.

Stopping all self-pity can be the start of a new and better life.

Instead of thinking, 'I am a victim,' start thinking, 'I have been made a stronger person because I survived all that awful stuff.'

Activity

1. Write in your journal about the bad things that were done to you. Include those 'small' things. They might well be very significant.

2. As you write and reflect on those bad things, think how they are now in your journal. They do not need to lead to self-pity.

3. Try writing, 'I survived and that has made me strong.' Put it up on your wall and think of all that strength you have.

25
Learning to be Realistic

If you don't believe in some kind of Designer, you have to believe in a whole huge number of improbable coincidences in order for life to have developed.

Russell Stannard

So much of our amazing little planet is ambiguous. It is about both 'bad' and 'good', about sadness and joy combined within the same thing. Life and death exist together – the seed dies so that the new plant can grow. It seems to me that it is this ambiguity that makes life so hard to deal with, yet also makes it so rich and interesting.

So, people who go through a bad patch, or those who have had very difficult things to cope with in their life, or those who have to cope with great sadness, can often become more sensitive and caring people because of those 'bad' things happening. The 'bad' in some ways leads to 'good'. That is just the way it is in our world.

■ Life and death

The people of India and Bangladesh, for example, wait anxiously for the torrential rains of the monsoon to end the months of drought. As the rain falls, celebrations begin because the rain means life, growth, and the promise of a rice harvest. But often people die as the rain comes in torrents and the floods start. The monsoon brings both life and death.

Our humanness is inextricably linked with this ambiguity of life and death, good and bad, wanting to cope out there beyond the wall yet at the same time wanting to stay curled up safely behind the wall.

■ Understanding our puzzling world

Surviving out there beyond the wall could be easier if we try to understand some of this ambiguity, and if we try to see that many things are not quite what they seem to be.

One of the things I am learning in therapy is that in people and most real situations in our life, there is always a mixture of good and bad. I am finding it very hard to believe this and constantly go back to my 'safe' position I learnt as a child that I am utterly bad and that all the ills of the world, war, floods, earthquakes, starvation, everything is my fault. (This might strike you as rather silly, but such a level of paranoia did come through in talking to other people about their low self-esteem.)

Perhaps part of the skill of surviving out there beyond the wall is to accept that the world is a place of mystery and ambiguity.

■ Not being the victim

One of our reactions to the pain we get in our odd little world is to blame everyone for that pain without taking sufficient responsibility for it ourselves. Pain and grief happen to everyone, and often there is no blame (although sometimes there is – a drunk driver, for example; or selfish parents who use their children for their own ends – although they might only be repeating the abuse they suffered as children).

If we behave as a victim and keep on blaming, we become unpleasant to be with. It is that stinking mud again, sticking to us and making us repulsive.

■ Stop blaming!

One of the ways we might know we are ready to make a doorway in the wall is when we are able to stop blaming ourselves for everything. We at last become able to distinguish in our lives the difference between the inappropriate blame that might have been laid on us from childhood and the quite appropriate sense of sadness for the way that human life seems to be so much about wrongdoing.

We do not have to go any further than the breakfast news to see that human life is crammed full of sadness and pain, much of it suffered at the hands of other human beings.

The truth is there facing us from every newspaper headline. Humans have in their veins more than a little trace of bitterness, sin, unkindness and what earlier generations more easily called 'evil'. Ugly word that. It gives me the shivers. I makes me think of witches' covens, ghouls and ghosts, horror movies and being murdered in the shower.

It is more comfortable, though, to keep this view of human wretchedness as some grand world-wide idea than it is to think of the wrongs of the world as coming in part from me. I can feel outrage at the wars. I can silently feel aloof from the murders, rapes and robberies. I can even allow myself to feel quite charitable about those who get caught up in a life of crime after a mixed-up childhood – there but for the grace of God go I, and all that.

But somehow I need to see that every human does things wrong. Like any human being, we can be selfish and so on. For example, I know that today, when the rest of my family get up, it will be all too easy for me to be too busy to attend to their needs, to listen to my children, and to insist on doing what I want rather than what is best for everyone. If we are honest with ourselves, we know that greed, deceitfulness and selfishness are all a part of everyday life. It is all just so easy to put ourselves first.

But we must be sure to tell ourselves that those things we do that we wish we hadn't are not things that we are going to go on 'beating ourselves up' about. For most things, we did the best we could at the time and now that is all in the past. Let the blame and the recrimination go. As the saying goes, 'Today is the first day of the rest of our lives.' Each new day is a day to do something positive and beautiful – but only if we ditch the blame!

■ Beyond blame

It seems that one of the things that can prevent us making that door in the wall is the wrong belief in our own wickedness. We feel such a sense of shame that we hide behind the wall.

We do not need to sit inside the tower to protect the world from our wickedness – or whatever reason we give for deciding not to make a doorway in the wall. Every human being has value and if we can just get ourselves beyond the blaming stage, we might feel able to make that hole in the wall into a door and start to come and go as we choose.

Blame and shame are two things that keep us in the tower. If we can work our way beyond both of those emotions, we can make the door and start to pull together the rest of our lives and be able to smile more.

Positive Pointers

We are free to make choices in our life.

We need not behave like victims.

Activity

Practise doing a 'freeze frame'. In the same way we can freeze the video to look at something for a longer time to see what it is really about, so we can learn to 'freeze frame' instead of freaking out when some crisis comes.

When rage, depressive negativity or whatever strikes us we can choose not to go down that chaotic and negative route and take it out on those around us.

1. Freeze.

2. Tell yourself that you do not need to do this negative junk.

3. Think carefully about what your immediate need is. It could be needing someone to listen, needing a cup of tea, or a hug, or chocolate, or needing to sit quietly with your teddy and looking through your special box until you feel that life can be coped with really. (It just doesn't feel like that rather a lot of the time.)

4. If anyone else is around, you can tell them what you need *calmly*. (I am working on that bit!)

Part 6

Living Beyond the Wall
Some of the Time

26
Healthy Relationships

You cannot enjoy full health as an isolated, separate being. Health is wholeness and wholeness implies connectedness – to family, friends, tribe, nation, humanity, the earth and whatever higher power you conceive to be the creator of the universe.

Andrew Weil

This next section is about making a permanent doorway in the wall so that we can choose to come and go easily and also make space for others in our life if we want that.

We are people in relation to others and inescapably (unless we become a hermit) we are part of networks and communities. Some networks are destructive and abusive, but others are creative and healing.

With a doorway we will always be able to go back behind the brick wall and build up our security by making time for our inner life to grow.

If we were to make a little hole in our wall and then make that into a door, we could get in and out reasonably easily. People could also get in. For some of us, both of these options are hard.

We do not have to make space for someone else. We do have a choice. But much of being human is about being people in relation to others, even if it is just the friendly face at the local chocolate shop.

Some of the people I have talked to who experience low self-esteem also say that they are lonely. There is a real problem here. There is the feeling of being uncomfortable around others, the fear of being exposed, so we hide away, but there is also the pull to be with others to overcome the loneliness. We are inescapably part of networks and communities.

■ Creative communities

One problem in some Western societies is that we are all such individuals and we do not live enough within communities and within the wider family. The 'Thatcherism' of 1980s Britain is responsible for some of this unhelpful shift from community to isolated individual, and we lack the support and sense of community that can be found in cultures where we would be more likely to live within the wider family.

Within some relationships and communities there is a huge amount of love and creativity. Like many other people, I feel great when I am being creative. I think that is because when we create, we are our most God-like.

It was one of my great heroes of creativity, William Morris, who said we should have nothing in our home that we do not believe to be beautiful or know to be useful, and this seems a good way to live out our lives, inside or outside the wall.

Creativity is taking what we have – friends, an idea, a lump of clay, a patch of earth or whatever – and making something from it that is either beautiful, or useful, or both. That can be a relationship, love, a song, a poem, a pizza, or a crop of beans.

The loss of community prevents us realising our potential as individuals.

Tony Blair

■ Healing communities

On a larger scale, we can help to create communities that are healing places:

■ the school where everyone, whatever their age and status, is treated with respect and valued for themselves, not just for what they contribute

157

- **the home where we know we are welcome**

- **the doctor's surgery where we are always treated with care**

- **the charity we support where we feel valued and where we can give of ourselves to others to be a part of their healing community.**

Sometimes just a moment of kindness from others can bring healing:

- **the shop where we are greeted with a smile**

- **the library where there is a quiet calm and someone who smiles as we check out our books.**

Many of the people I talked to about their low self-esteem felt very isolated and lonely. It seemed to me that their need was to be a part of some kind of 'healing community' even if this was only for a very short time. Some of them said that belonging to a self-help group was a real lifeline.

■ Changes we can make

When we get into some kind of destructive event or relationship, we can often find ourselves trying to change something that it is not in our power to change.

This is a pointless thing to try to do.

> **God, give us grace to accept with serenity the things that cannot be changed, courage to change the things that should be changed, and the wisdom to distinguish the one from the other.**
>
> Reinhold Niebuhr

If we are setting out to try to change something we cannot change we are destined for yet more failure. Equally, if we just sit and watch something going wrong that we really do have the power to change, we are not making the effort that we could in order to make our lives, and those of the people around us, a bit more comfortable.

■ We can change ourselves

In any breakdown of relationships it seems to me that some kind of healing could take place if we start with our own willingness to move from an entrenched position – usually that we are right and they are wrong!

That we can change ourselves is something we need to cling on to as we seek to move from our deeply held beliefs about our own shame and unworthiness, to a position where our self-esteem starts to blossom and we are a bit more realistic and positive about ourselves.

> ■ Through negotiation we can also change our work roles both in and out of the home.

> ■ We can change how we use our time and money and our attitude to them.

> ■ We can change our hobbies and choose to develop our talents more.

> ■ We can change our outlook on life, our goals and ambitions.

> ■ We can change our fitness and to some extent the overall shape and size of our body.

> ■ We can choose to develop ourselves more within our wider family and community.

We can even change our hopes and dreams into reality and there is more about this in later chapters.

This week I changed one aspect of my life for the better. I went to a kennels and chose a little puppy. She is my Annie and already I adore her. I know I have taken a big risk – if we let ourselves risk love, we can end up hurt. But not to risk love is to be too feeble. Too unwilling to get out there beyond the wall. She is utterly beautiful and I feel more complete with a dog to relate to.

Positive Pointers

Decide to move on from things that happened in the past.

Speak up for those in your community who need help. It will make you feel good and they will feel they have a friend.

Activity

You could try making two lists. One of the things we can change and one of things we just have to live with.

These are things that we probably cannot change:

■ **getting older**

■ **our children leaving home**

■ **our family background and history**

■ **becoming ill**

■ **the death of someone we love (not 'loved', because we go on loving them, that is the problem)**

■ **abuse by someone older/stronger/more powerful than us (actually abuse could go in both lists)**

■ **our natural face shape, bone structure, etc. (This could be changed to some extent by plastic surgery, but I am putting it in the 'cannot change' list because for most of us we just have to learn to live with ourselves the way we are.)**

These are things we might be able to change:

■ **the way in which we dress**

■ **the care we take of our body**

■ **the way we treat people**

■ **our attitude to those around us, for example we can learn to forgive**

■ **the people we spend time with.**

And so on.

Think of the list above about the things that we can change and select just one thing, for example a hobby you could take up, and set aside some time to realize a dream.

Without the humility and warmth which you have to develop in your relations to the few with whom you are personally involved, you will never be able to do anything for the many.

Dag Hammerskjold

27
Taking Time for Inner Life

> Although I'm not religious I'm quite spiritual. The
> big band and I always share a spiritual moment before
> a concert. We stand round in a circle while someone
> says a few words to bring us together. It's a sort of
> thank you, an acknowledgement of whichever god
> you happen to believe in. I do believe that someone,
> somewhere, is probably keeping count.
>
> Phil Collins

As we try to develop our self-esteem and creep out into the
world sometimes we find that we must look after many
different aspects of ourselves if we are really going to make
some permanent change and become more confident.

If we ignore deep bits inside us, we are not allowing ourselves
to be fully human and develop all of our potential. We have an
inner life of our dreams and hopes, our creativity, our thinking,
the things we long for, our deepest needs, and of course all those
unconscious things we only get a glimpse of now and then.

This is our inner life, and it needs developing and caring
for just in the way we look after our many other needs.

This could start to sound a bit too inward-looking and
selfish, but caring for and loving others are totally interwoven
with caring for and loving ourselves. To 'love our neighbour
as ourselves' is two aspects of love that need to be developed
together. Neglect one and we create havoc with the other.

Caring for ourselves goes alongside caring for others.

■ Getting a grip on life

When life feels as out of control as mine does at the moment,
I cannot contemplate getting a grip on all of it. What I can

do is just do something simple when I can. As I write in my journal I begin to unpack why it feels so overwhelming, then I can try to sort out the problem. But that is a huge task. I can only do it bit by bit, often taking many backward steps into the safety behind my brick wall.

Sometimes when I read books on self-esteem it feels as if other people can manage life, but I cannot, so I must be totally hopeless. I hate those books of the 12-simple-steps-to-manage-your-life type. I do the 12 steps, but I am just the same. I think it is partly because they are not *simple* steps. Changing how we think and feel is terribly difficult and can only happen over quite a bit of time.

■ Feeling real feelings

For real change to happen involves us changing the inner messages that we give ourselves and this means that we need to focus on our inner life – and that is difficult in itself. If you are like me you will be very good at finding ways to block out any difficult feelings deep down inside. This ability to 'space out' is one thing I can honestly say I am an expert in!

It is all too easy to neglect our inner life in the rush and demands of ordinary living. I deliberately keep life at a rush so I can more effectively block out the uncomfortable inner feelings.

■ We are spiritual beings

I know many people who have rejected any kind of spiritual aspect to their lives. Some of them insist there is no such thing as our soul. Some say there is no God. Some tell sad stories of things that happened to them which have given them a reason to reject God.

But the problem with a total rejection of everything spiritual is that, as someone put it, we have a 'God-shaped vacuum' in our lives. We can try to fill this hole with things other than God, but like those children's shape-posting toys, only one shape will go in the hole. We can try all our lives to post food, drink, loud music, sex, chocolate and all kinds of worthy and relaxing hobbies that we love into the God-shaped hole, but they just will not fit the need.

We do not need to become terribly holy or wear hair shirts or stand on street corners yelling about the Bible. (Organized religion comes pretty near the top of my list of things I really don't much care for!) But we need to try to let that spiritual bit of ourselves out and let it soar.

■ A God-shaped hole

I see the God-shape hole as that ordinary human longing for some kind of recognition of the spiritual. We see that human longing around us as a mother pulls a bough of blossom towards her child to wonder at the beauty of it. We see it as we stand in front of a great work of art, or when we see someone we love walk through the door and smile at us. To me there is something about life that is much more than the molecules of the universe and the biological behaviour patterns of humans. I think there is another 'layer' that is about love and creativity, about belonging, about caring and about that leap within us when we see the first snowdrop of spring and know that the death and devastation of winter will soon be over.

I think we get close to filling that God-shaped hole if we try to fill the empty longing in our lives with something creative. But unless we try to get a grip on the real problem of our God-shaped hole, nothing else but a recognition that we are spiritual beings is going to help. If we ignore that inner longing we are doomed to a life of knowing somehow that we have something missing.

■ Nurturing our soul

But there is another way to look at this. If we don't recognize and nurture our spiritual life within us, a bit of us is being unused and starts to wither and I have wondered if this contributes to our low self-esteem. There is a bit of us that is uncared for, but if we were to recognize it, care for it, smile at it, maybe that bit of us would begin to thrive and grow. It is a valuable bit of what makes us truly our unique selves.

So, if we were to say, 'Yes, I am a spiritual being and, yes, I will feed and nurture that bit of me', maybe we will begin to feel better about ourselves and gradually change some of our perceptions of ourselves. Just as caring for our physical body can improve our self-esteem, so nurturing our spirit in some way could have the same effect.

What I mean is:

■ Being creative. (Make an attractive meal, paint, garden, write, sew, make a geometric pattern, put up a shelf, do some patchwork.)

■ Taking time to enjoy the natural world. (Make a butterfly garden, go for a walk, grow flowers and a favourite vegetable or herb.)

■ Meditating and developing a sense of quietness and meaning inside ourselves.

■ Resting our bodies and recognizing that our general well-being depends of many different ways of relaxing and finding a sense of inner peace.

■ Being with people we enjoy, or ringing them up and letting ourselves both give and receive positive messages from them.

■ Caring for others. (Listening to others, helping a charity with money or with our time, visiting friends and family, making a cup of tea for someone we love.)

These are the kinds of things that help us to see we are not just a bundle of molecules adrift in a huge universe and the accidental product of some chaotic evolutionary process.

It all seems so pointless if, when we die, we rot and nothing else. I believe that our spirit lives on. What we have done, who we are, and the influences that we have had on the lives of others goes on whether these were positive and good things or nasty and vicious things that penetrate into the next generation leaving a good or a bitter taste many years after we have died.

Positive Pointer

Let your soul out! Give it the freedom to soar.

Activity

Over the next few weeks try out a variety of things to develop your inner life. To get you started here are some things I am doing at the moment:

■ **Taking a minute to relax completely by tensing up each bit of my body in turn and then relaxing it so that at the end of the minute all my body is flopping and at rest. You can try to build this up gradually so that you relax totally for five minutes.**

■ **Sitting quietly with my journal trying to write down some of what I am thinking so that I can understand why I am so spaced out at the moment. Yesterday I managed to do this for almost 10 minutes which is the longest time for about three months. Something had happened in therapy that really upset me and I knew I was angry because I felt misunderstood. That seemed to get me going so I am seeing it was good that I could connect with my feelings of anger and focus on them.**

■ **Meditating for a few minutes when I can. This is desperately hard, but I am spending lots of time in the garden at the moment, so I am trying to turn some sentences to God when I see my baby lettuces growing and my snapdragon seedlings peeping through the soil. I am also reading some Celtic prayers. These are short, related to the world around me, and I find them totally unthreatening.**

My body is as tense as a cat's
    As it stalks its prey.
Lord, relax my body.
    My thoughts swirl like willow branches
Caught in autumn winds.
    Lord, still my thoughts.
My soul is as heavy as peat
    Freshly dug from the bog.
Lord, lighten my soul.
    My heart is as dark as soil
Sodden with the winter rains.
    Lord, brighten my heart.

From *Celtic Prayers*, Robert Van de Weyer

28
Looking After Our Body

**I can feel depressed and then dance to music, then
I feel a million dollars. Life does not have to hurt.**

A woman on TV

I have noticed that some people with low self-esteem can
tend not to bother to take care of themselves. That isn't
always true of course, but for many of us there seems no
point in bothering.

■ Why bother to wash my hair before I go out – it always looks
dreadful anyway.

■ Why bother to put cream on my hands? How can it matter if they
are all cracked and dry?

■ Why bother to get all dressed up in neat, clean clothes? I am just
who I am – a crumpled dishevelled wreck.

But if we are to survive out there beyond the brick wall, taking
some care of ourselves seems to make us feel better. These can
be very simple and varied things and do not need to cost much
money.

■ Buying something from a charity shop can help us to feel good.
Last week I bought a really great men's shirt to go with my jeans.
It cost less than a packet of chocolate biscuits and it is long enough
to cover my wobbly bits.

■ I am getting stressed and depressed at the moment so I am
borrowing taped stories from the library and playing those on
journeys to take my mind off therapy.

■ I read in a list of advice about how to distract yourself from overeating that buying yourself flowers can help you to feel you value yourself so much that you won't eat that incredibly delicious packet of freshly baked double-chocolate-chip cookies. I need some convincing about this. I have tried it a few times and it seems to work. My kitchen window sill has several different coloured African violets – but I have also had cookies sometimes.

■ It is all or nothing

I find my phases of caring about myself rarely last more than a few weeks before the 'What's the point' stuff gets to the top again. As long as I am caring about all aspects of myself, I can keep to it, but as soon as something slips, the whole lot goes. I then spend weeks hardly bothering to think about anything to do with caring for my body.

But I have found something very important. I can reverse all this just by getting one thing going again. So if I am really trying hard to lose a bit of weight by keeping off things with a high fat content, I generally find I will keep to that if I am also taking time to go to the gym, brush my hair, not drive myself into the ground with work and also am bothering to rub cream into my skin. (For some reason bits of my skin seem to be metamorphosing into sandpaper good enough to rub down the kitchen table before I revarnish it.)

So making the effort to do one thing often means I will bother to do other things and get myself into a good and caring phase.

■ Caring for our body

These are things that we can think of as caring for our body:

- ■ healthy eating
- ■ some kind of exercise
- ■ build in various kinds of relaxation.

169

■ A healthy diet

I feel better if I eat lots of fresh fruit and vegetables, keep off junk and processed food and keep mostly to low-fat foods. I say mostly because I know it is good to have a set of rules to restrict what we eat and many people take the rule of never eating anything with more than five per cent fat. Yes, I can see the sense in it, and mostly I do it. But to do it all the time would mean that I could never eat humus, or real ice-cream, or chocolate or make a cheese pizza with loads of mozzarella and maybe another cheese as well.

So I think that provided we keep to a reasonably healthy diet, it just isn't realistic to think of never having some of the things we love – unless our life depends on it. Things in this world are for us to enjoy, and anyway, the minute I think I will have no chocolate all this week, I spend so much time thinking that I cannot have it that I think about it so much, I end up having it and maybe too much of it!

If we feel deprived of something, we just want it all the more!

There are dozens of books about healthy eating and dozens more about what to avoid to keep your hips and thighs trim, what not to eat with protein, what not to eat if you are blood type O, what vitamin supplement to take if you want to have the energy of an eight-year-old, and what to take to keep your arteries from blocking up, and so on.

We could go crazy if we tried to take all the advice there is around, so I have come to a position where I have some basic rules for what I eat:

■ I do not eat meat. I eat mostly fruit and vegetables.

■ I eat loads of yoghurt. (It keeps up the numbers of those essential little bugs we need in our intestines.)

■ I avoid all processed food. I get organic produce when I can. I grow favourite vegetables.

■ I take a magnifying glass with me to the shop and read the food labels. (OK, I admit that is verging on the slightly crazy, but I am not

one of these people who thinks looking as if you are sane is important.)
I rarely buy food with things in them that I don't think need to be
there. Try reading what is in some yoghurts!

**I made a few essential rules. I ate only low-fat foods.
I ate nothing between meals. I ate food I enjoy and
had wine... I knew I could keep to these few rules
and I did.**

Nigel Lawson, former chancellor of the exchequer

■ Exercise

■ Doing at least three sessions of at least 20 minutes each week is
about right – but if you are 80 you might want to do less! I try to do
some small exercise every day when I am feeling able to and about
an hour of more intense exercise three times a week.

■ It is important to start out very gently indeed and even more
important to go to your doctor for a check-up before you start.

■ Choose something you enjoy! Motivation is so important, so
involve a friend if that grabs you, or join a class.

Housework is great exercise, but as I do very little of this, I like
to do other things. I like going to the gym, swimming, cycling
and playing an exercise video. But walking briskly for half an
hour or dancing to a tape costs nothing and is very effective.

■ Relaxation

There are several different kinds of relaxation and we need
to find what we need and when we need it. I find that I need
different things at different times. If I am totally exhausted
and my body is screaming out for mercy, about all I can do
is sit in front of the television and watch a film. If I just need
time off from work, but am still capable of logical thought, I
like to sew and listen to the radio.

It is important to discover what it is that helps us to switch off completely from the world. I have learnt that sometimes I need just to stop completely and do absolutely nothing. I go to bed and shut my eyes.

■ Incentive

The key to all this looking after ourselves is that we need to find out what works for us. I am learning to listen more to my body, respect it, value it and care for it.

The problem is we find little incentive to do all this when we feel so bad about ourselves. But I heard a stunning thing recently that has boosted my incentive. I was told that our generation is going to live much longer than the previous one. Many of us will live well into our 80s or 90s. That will happen whether we like it or not!

So we can choose. We can look after ourselves and exercise and live out our final years fairly independently, able to look after ourselves and get ourselves to the loo and stay in our own home. Or we can be complete slobs now, let ourselves go and need to be looked after by those kind people who work in nursing homes and call everyone 'dearie', have to sit in the day room and play bingo and most worrying of all, lose our independence to do what we want, when we want, in the way we want.

It is enough to send you rushing out of the house to do a 10-mile brisk walk every day!

Positive Pointer

Exercise reduces stress, helps us to feel good and improves our general health.

Activity

---

1. Make your own list of rules for your eating, because what suits one person isn't right for another.

■ People do have food allergies and often these can be undetected unless we take time to have tests. Health food shops in my area offer these or ask around about herbalists or homeopaths.

■ Buying real food isn't necessarily expensive. Often it is the processed foods that cost so much, so browse around the fresh food.

2. Keeping some kind of food and exercise diary can help. You could:

■ write down everything you eat so that you get a sense of what you are consuming.

■ write a plan for what you will eat during a day.

■ hang a calendar up and mark on it days when you exercise.

■ give yourself gold stars for good eating and exercise days. (This really does work!)

Don't give up!

■ Even five minutes' gentle exercise walking to the shops helps.

■ If you have had a bad food day/week/month/lifetime, it is never too late to decide to eat healthily.

Be realistic:

■ Of course you are going to have bad days. Everyone does. Just pick yourself up and start again. (If only it were that easy!)

3. Remember to say, 'Well done,' to yourself!

Part 7

Dealing with Bulldozers

29
Surviving in a Tough World

A journal can help you figure out how you feel, what you think, what you need, what you want to say, how you want to handle a situation, just by writing it through.

Ellen Bass and Laura Davis, *The Courage to Heal*

This section is about our need to learn to deal with 'bulldozer' people who are out there in the world and who seem not to care whom they knock down.

For some of us who experience low self-esteem, the world is a very frightening place and we just cannot manage it. We take cover behind our brick wall, the only place where we feel safe. But, to our horror, the world out there has powerful 'bulldozer' people charging about, not caring if they knock down walls, or worrying about who they hurt in the process. They stay in a state of 'very annoyed rhinoceros' whenever anything goes even slightly wrong. Their aim seems to be to get in front of everyone and get the better of everyone, no matter what the cost.

Unfortunately, the world is rather full of these bulldozer people. Our society seems to foster brashness and encourage those who want to get exactly what they want, riding roughshod over everyone and everything that dares to get in their way.

■ The world is a pushy place

As I drive across London twice a week to go to therapy, I find it quite extraordinary how many drivers seem completely obsessed with being in front of me.

Why is it so important to be in front? They practically sit

on my back bumper until there is a space, then shoot past, risking my life, their life and the lives of the startled people in the car coming the other way. Is it really worth risking several lives just to get five metres in front? I cannot believe that all the people who do it are on life or death missions. Anyway, when they are forced to stop at the next traffic lights, I often catch them up anyway because I plod along in the inside lane and they go in the outside lane, only to get held up by someone who is turning. So they are behind me again and then the whole process starts all over again.

What strikes me as so odd about this is that there are so many of these aggressive drivers and I wonder if this is the way they run their lives – always needing to be ahead and not really caring what they do to get there. As an attitude to life, I cannot see that as being very helpful.

■ Coping with being knocked down

Most of us experience bulldozers demolishing our wall of safety at some time or other. I used to work for someone who just rode rough-shod over everyone and it was one of the worst experiences of my life. But what is so surprising now, is that I have recovered from it. When I talk to others who experience bulldozers, they do mostly talk of recovery, and that is important.

We need to believe that bulldozers do not rule the world.

We can get our wall back up. It is completely appropriate to do that. We can then get back to our safe position behind it and recover from the experience.

■ Fear of being abandoned

For many people, fear of being abandoned is a huge underlying fear and one of the major things that can bring the brick wall crashing down. Many people expressed their fear of abandonment to me in a whole variety of ways, and because it is one of my really big, mega, monster, scary things, I recognized it in others who didn't mention it.

Our sense that we will be abandoned is another one of those 'inner child' things we must allow ourselves to feel. We probably felt abandoned as babies if our mother just went out of the room and didn't deliver lunch exactly when we wanted it. To a baby, if mum isn't there, she has disappeared out of the universe and that must be very scary indeed.

■ Feelings around death

Death is, I suppose, the ultimate form of being abandoned, and as I sat with my mother last week as she died, I was surprised how calm I felt. I think I had worked through the feelings of her leaving us all, and the thought that I might feel terrible guilt, and be plunged into months of grief.

In the end it was all a huge relief to see her escape from a life in which she was not very happy. So instead of being completely knocked over, as I had expected, I discovered that it just is not possible to predict how we will react to a big 'life event'.

As I had thought, I was much less upset than when my dog Jemma died, because working through feelings and talking about them seems to have the effect that they are less powerful and not so overwhelming. (Now, *that* is a lesson for all of us!)

You will probably have gathered that my mother was the main 'bulldozer' person in my life. She terrified me. But it has been very good in the last few months of her life as she lay dying, to share my new puppy Annie with her and just sit and hold her hand.

It was a little bit tempting to do the bulldozer thing back to her! I was now the one with the power, and wow! Did that feel good!

But I felt so very sorry for her. The only thing that made her smile was Annie jumping on her and licking her face enthusiastically. Bulldozers can be very lonely people who do not know any other way to treat people. If they are like my mother, they have not got their aims, ambitions and dreams sorted out. They really do not know what life is actually about beyond the level of keeping themselves alive and acquiring possessions.

So maybe bulldozers could be less destructive in our lives if we see that they can be the saddest of people who only knock us down because they do not know a better way to communicate with us.

■ Low expectations

I think one of the reasons I became a teacher was because that was what my mother expected of me. And I hadn't been a teacher very long before I realized that the expectations we have of children profoundly influence what the children actually achieve.

There are some social research stories around of teachers being given a class of average or mixed achievers and being told that all the children are high achievers. Other teachers in the school are given a class of similar ability, but are told that they are all the low achievers. (I happen to think that this is unethical. No research should prejudice a child's education, but the stories make a point.) Then at the end of the term or year the children are all tested, and surprise, surprise! All the children that the teachers were told were bright get really good marks, and all the children who the teachers were told were lower achievers (but who actually had the same ability) did very badly.

■ We get what we expect to get

It seems that low expectations can work the same for our own inner world. If we sit around believing all the junk we have picked up along the way about being no good, and expect 'bulldozer' people to knock us over, guess what? They will knock us over.

But the fantastically good bit about this is that we can change that for ourselves.

■ We can have higher expectations of ourselves. ('I'm getting stronger emotionally and I'm really going to set out to make my life more positive and stop believing all those "old tapes".')

■ We can work at strategies for how to dodge the bulldozers. ('I'm going to just walk away if he starts on at me. I'm not going to let him bully me in that way.')

■ We can develop strategies to build ourselves up again. ('Just because I fell apart yesterday doesn't mean that today will be a bad day as well. I'm going to look after myself by meditating for a few minutes, then I'm going to get on with today's list of things to do.')

Positive Pointer

If we expect more from ourselves, we achieve more.

Activity

1. Write down some of your 'bulldozer' people or situations. List next to them what it is that makes you so vulnerable near those people, or so nervous in that situation.

Now, over the next few weeks, try to work on what you wrote. The crucial things to remember about bulldozers are:

■ It might take some time, but we can pick ourselves up and learn to cope with them.

■ People who behave in that intimidating way are often trying to defend their own vulnerability.

■ Those who are just aggressive thugs need our pity – we are much more sensitive people who care about others and can help others who are suffering.

2. Picture a person wearing a T-shirt with 'Handle with care. Valuable human being' on it.

Part 8

Dismantling the Wall

30
Building a New and Better Wall

The smallest act of kindness is worth more than the grandest intentions. Who, being loved, is poor?
Oscar Wilde

This section is about us taking some control over our lives. We can choose to dismantle the wall if we want, or keep it, but make a door, or we can use the bricks to build something else.

We need to be realistic about what we can achieve, but equally, we need to expect more from ourselves and try to follow our dreams and ambitions.

As we progress and become more confident and positive and begin to be able to value ourselves, we can choose to change our protective wall, maybe even knock it down, or to keep it and make it better, perhaps with a good-sized door in it and a bay window.

Then we could use some of the spare bricks to make a barbecue for summer parties, a kiln to bake our pottery attempts, or cover bricks with material and make them into book ends. All of these things are constructive and about our new life of creativity that we are working our way towards.

Or we could use the spare bricks as ammunition to throw at bulldozer people who annoy us. This would be a fairly negative thing to do – but sometimes we do need to express our anger and frustration at the world.

■ We live on our defences

The reason we built the wall in the first place was because we were hurt and frightened and we needed to have some protection and firm defences in order to consider staying alive. We might even have made it into a tower that completely surrounded us and which no one else could penetrate. But we built it quickly and without any planning, so we might well want to take it down and build it with a better foundation because, useful though the tower is, it can become a bit of a prison.

I think it is inappropriate to take down the wall completely because we do need some kind of defences to live. Everyone does, not just those who find life gruelling.

■ Wearing masks

People talk about us having masks that we wear in order to hide our real selves and I thoroughly approve of this idea. Some people hint that we do not need to wear these masks, but I think we do. I might well be getting more confident, but I need my brick wall and a lot of hooks on which I can hang my various masks!

Anyway, if we are to be out there in the world and also conscious of our need to have appropriate boundaries, we need masks most desperately when our boundaries are invaded.

■ It is absolutely right for us to decide that we will only come out of our hiding place when we choose.

■ We can wear any masks we choose to and keep things that we do not want to share to ourselves.

■ We can change these masks when we want and take them off when we want.

Don't forget that we can have a very confident mask for days when we need it. If we have to do something difficult, it is often very useful to try to appear more confident than we feel inside. And remembering that if we behave in a confident way, that is part of what we need to do to learn to be more confident in the long term.

■ Finding our deepest wants and needs

If we are to become more at peace with ourselves and the world around us we need to take time to work out what our deepest wants and needs are. Again, this sounds self-centred, but it need not be. Some of my deepest wants and needs are to nurture, love and care for my children and partner. Others are to find time three or four times a week just to be silent, and other times to get some exercise at the gym.

■ Finding our 'true self'

We will be finding out about what some psychologists call our 'true self' as we work at discovering more about ourselves. For example:

- ■ what we really want to do with our lives

- ■ as we write in our journal

- ■ as we find people of a like mind and a positive outlook to be with

- ■ if we maybe join a self-help group

- ■ if we find some other group to belong to.

Psychologists also talk about the 'false self' which is when we are in our dysfunctional relationships, when we are terrified to face the world, when we are trying to be our parent's perfect child. The false us is the bits of us that just are not coping with life. It is us listening to our 'old tapes' instead of being more realistic and seeing ourselves as worthwhile and valuable human beings.

Our 'true self' is our complete person, body, mind and spirit – if you can split people up like that. It is as we let our inner life grow and flourish that we get in touch with:

- ■ what we really feel (painful!).

- ■ what we really want to do with our life (essential).

We come to understand who we really are and how we can defeat those feelings of low self-esteem (absolutely magic when it happens).

■ Being happy

If we believe that our happiness is dependent on other people, we are in real trouble. Waiting for the longed-for perfect partner, friends, money, career or whatever is a hopeless wait.

We are also not being fair to ourselves and our inner life. If we constantly wait for happiness just to come to us from somewhere in the cosmos, we are looking in the wrong place. Happiness is something that has to start inside us and I know it is very hard to understand. It took me a long time to get to the start of seeing that my happiness is dependent on me and my attitudes. I thought I 'ought' to be happy when I had a tiny baby, a lovely partner, a home and so on. But I wasn't.

I now understand that our happiness is about the things in this book:

■ really making a top priority to understand our inner life

■ guarding our personal space with determination and good humour

■ leading a life in which we nurture both ourselves and those around us

■ valuing others

■ forgiving ourselves and others

■ being true to ourselves and our beliefs

■ allowing our spiritual world to flourish

■ accepting ourselves

■ learning to trust both ourselves and those we love

■ loving ourselves unconditionally.

In other words, we have the power to be happy within ourselves and I know that thought can be very disconcerting at first. But the longer we sit around waiting for happiness to arrive at our front door one day, the longer we are wasting time at achieving our dream of happiness now.

■ Hopes, dreams and ambitions

To lose our hopes and dreams is to me when we start getting old. It is so inspiring to see elderly people on the television doing something like running a marathon (one of my hopes), or skydiving out of an airplane, or seeing someone doing a wonderful job being a creative and loving grandparent.

I think it is important to be realistic about what we want to do and who we want to be and so on, but we also need to find ways to do those things we long to do.

■ Peace and justice

As human beings, part of our building a new and better wall is to lift our eyes beyond our own small world and ask ourselves what we can do for our planet and the six billion people on it. Our hopes, dreams and ambitions can be global, not just limited to our small part of the world.

I find it inspiring to hear people at the United Nations talking about working to halve poverty in 10 years and eliminate it in a few more years; to end wars; to bring peace and justice to our planet. It has to be right to think like that and not to believe the skeptical journalists who tell UN officials that they are being unreal.

How can we live at peace with ourselves in the rich Western world when hundreds of homeless people walk the streets of New York and London? When wars rage and bring devastation to families who are caught up in them? When a huge number of children in India cannot go to school because they are the family breadwinner? It would be a massive project to get every child in India into school – it would need thousands more schools and teachers for a start, but to strive for anything less seems to deny children a creative and fulfilled life.

Yes, of course we need to be realistic, but society never got any better because people just said the task ahead was too big to contemplate. It is by having the vision and the dream for what could be, combined with breaking a huge problem down into small manageable bits that change for the better takes place.

Imagine what would have happened if Ghandi or Florence Nightingale had decided the problem was too big for them so they would just ignore it.

It seems to me that, in terms of justice, there is no reason why people should go hungry these days other than the greed of those who do not, and corrupt political systems. One of the reasons I don't eat meat is about justice. I was told that if we didn't feed such huge quantities of grain to beef cattle in the West, there would be plenty of grain to fill the bowls of the hungry.

Hunger, war, homelessness, the rape of our planet, and all that terrifying stuff is not something 'out there'. It concerns us as feeling creative people with hopes, dreams and ambitions for a better world.

You have not done enough, you have never done enough, so long as it is still possible that you have something to contribute.

Dag Hammerskjold

Positive Pointers

We can all find ways to help society.

We can all find ways to help to protect our planet.

We can all dream dreams and try to fulfil them.

List some of those things that you used to want to do. Which ones could you still do if you really made the effort?

O Great Creator, Father of all people, we commit to you the needs of the whole world. Where there is hatred will you bring forth love; where there is injury, grant your pardon, Lord; where there is distrust, will you restore faith and bring back a spirit of child-like trust; where there is sorrow, will you bring the peace of deep joy; where there is darkness, let there be your glorious light. Through Jesus Christ our Saviour and Redeemer. Amen.

Based on a prayer by St Francis of Assisi

31
Living a Creative Life

We need to expect more from ourselves. We tend easily to set limits on ourselves... We could all do more to see some of our dreams come true.

Linda Finch

Once we can cope without being behind our wall most of the time, we discover that the world out there can be very exciting and interesting. There are all kinds of opportunities to be creative and compassionate, even if we have very little money or very little time. And letting our lives be more creative, we understand our inner life better, so we can raise our self-esteem and feel that we are OK as a person.

■ Using our gifts

Being creative doesn't mean you have to learn to paint. It means:

- **presenting meals attractively.**

- **having hobbies or a job where we can make things.**

- **creating thoughts and ideas in the minds of others.**

- **spreading joy and peace by saying kind things.**

Creating things can give us so much satisfaction that it feeds into our inner world and we feel pleased and proud of what we have done. That is the boost to our self-esteem.

I would go so far as to say that if we don't include something creative in our life we are needlessly trapping ourselves in low self-esteem. But we have to plan to be creative. Like happiness, it isn't just going to descend on us one day.

People often talk to me about wanting to be a writer. Some say they would be if only they could find the time. Some say they are waiting for inspiration to strike them. But being a writer isn't like that. I have to find the time and if I sat about waiting for inspiration before I wrote anything I would never get books done. It is the 'bum-on-chair' stuff that gets books written. It is as I sit here, and as I reflect on my work as I drink cups of tea and so on, that the words actually get on the page.

■ Making a plan to be creative

Your situation will be different from mine, but here are some ideas that you could plan for:

■ Visit an elderly neighbour.

■ Start a babysitting circle.

■ Invite all the neighbours in to help you get the garden ready for a barbecue.

■ Send a loving postcard to a long-lost friend.

■ Draw up a family tree to share with the family.

■ Find all the old photos of your grandparents and make copies for all your nieces and nephews.

■ Buy junk furniture and paint it rainbow colours with those little trial pots of paint from DIY shops.

■ Run a short story competition to support your favourite charity.

■ Teach something to a child, for example how to build a small wildlife pond out of a plastic dustbin.

These things won't just happen. We have to make a plan. It is a plan to be a different person in a few months time – a more positive person – someone who is good to have around. Someone who has come out from behind their wall and is now making a difference to the community in which they live.

■ What is the point of it all?

Be not so busy making a living that you forget to make a life.

I have a card with this saying up in the kitchen where I can see it every day. It means a great deal to me because it keeps me focused on what the point of it all is, and it keeps me aware that many people do not have a job and they would very much like to have paid work as I do.

But I can all too easily get carried away with the rather boring and sometimes uncreative educational things that earn money and forget the other more creative things that I want to do that don't bring in money.

I have a son, a godson, a niece and a nephew who are all either in or heading towards life in the arts. How brave these young people are and how much I admire them. They learnt young that to follow your dreams is a way to a happy and fulfilled life. They brushed aside that well-meaning, but hopelessly misguided, advice from some of the adults around them to 'Get a proper job' and 'Go in for a safe career where you have good prospects and a good steady income.'

Sometimes it seems that wisdom is not something that comes with age, but it is about knowing how to follow your dreams for your short life here on earth.

Having enough money to live on is not about having lots of it, but knowing that you can manage without very much of it.

Jonathan Atkinson

■ I want to make pots

I want to tell you a story that I heard a long time ago:

191

There was once a potter who had his own small pottery where he made and sold beautiful pots. One day the potter was sitting outside his pottery having his lunch of bread and cheese and enjoying sitting in the sun and watching the birds.

A tourist came to the pottery and was admiring the pots and he noticed that they were very cheap compared with similar pots back in his own country. The tourist was a businessman and he went up to the potter and said,

'Do you make all these pots yourself?'

'I do', said the potter.

'You know if you had an assistant you could make many more of these pots.'

'Why would I want to do that?' asked the potter.

'Well, you could export them because you could sell hundreds of these pots where I come from.'

'Why would I want to do that?' asked the potter.

'Well, you could make lots of money', said the tourist.

'Why would I want to do that?' asked the potter.

'Well, you could employ more assistants and leave them to make all the pots.'

'Why would I want to do that?' asked the potter.

'Well, you could then live a more relaxed life and sit and rest in the sun.'

'Like I'm doing now, you mean?' asked the potter.

'Well, yes, I suppose so', said the tourist, 'but you would make lots more money.'

'But I don't want to make money,' said the potter, 'I want to make pots.'

It is all too easy in our materialistic culture to focus our lives on money. But it is a trap that can rob us of a sense of what is important in life.

Yes, having paid employment can boost our self-esteem. Yes, it is wonderful to be able to afford to buy organic vegetables that taste so good and buy a new pair of shoes when we need them. But life isn't really about those things. Getting some sense of perspective on what is really important in life can make us happier people, because we will be more contented and fulfilled.

■ Aiming for the really important things in life

I want to go on exploring the part of me that I will call my soul; the bit of me that surges with emotion when King Lear wants revenge, when Ophelia goes mad, when I see a golden eagle soar down the glen, when I hold a newborn baby in my arms, and when someone I love hugs me.

I see this soul as the core of our being. It is the bit that is transformed when we let our creativity out; when we 'let go' and allow ourselves to join in with the part of our universe that goes far beyond the physical world; when we start to accept that we are accepted by the Great Creator because of the immeasurable greatness of his love.

Positive Pointers

We are unique as well as special. We have unique features, finger prints, dreams, hopes and ambitions.

Defeating inertia and 'just doing it' is one sure way to raise self-esteem.

Activity

1. Brainstorm with a friend some of the things that you might be able to do to become more creative.

2. If you like the idea of a special box to boost you during the low points in your life, how about starting one off for someone else who is finding life tough at the moment?

3. Or become a postcard sender. Just the briefest of messages are needed with a good picture to help someone feel that they are special and that you are thinking about them.

4. Think of the most wonderful person you know. Why is he or she so great? List the things that you admire. Then set about developing those things in yourself.

Part 9

What Now?

32
Getting Beyond the Fear

A man is happy so long as he chooses to be happy and nothing can stop him.

Alexander Solzhenitsyn

This final section is about what we do once we have found that living beyond the wall is manageable at least for some of the time.

We will now have a much more secure building around us and a more secure understanding of who we are and what we really want out of life.

I am beginning to feel those really good feelings of thinking and feeling that I am OK really. I was trying to explain them to Ruth this morning. It is like those unexpected feelings I had when I worked with John, 10 years ago now – suddenly and apparently from nowhere I began to feel good about myself.

This morning it felt as if there were some magical blanket surrounding me and I was warm and comfortable and secure as I tried to explain how sometimes, in fleeting moments, I can feel that I'm an OK person. I can feel it deep down within myself.

■ We are a mixture of good and bad

I have been trying so hard not to keep putting myself down and trying to be more realistic about myself. I am back to that really crucial thing of trying to believe that I am not a completely hopeless and bad person who doesn't deserve space on God's earth. Like everyone else I am a mixture of good and bad, and just because I don't get it right all the time, it doesn't mean I am useless.

Explaining the good feelings to Ruth, it felt as if they might suddenly fly away and be gone for ever. It is intriguing how logic seems to have nothing to do with what we feel sometimes.

Ruth understood my wandering thoughts. This was one of those moments in therapy when the good bits at last balance out all the struggles and pain that therapy can bring. I knew it was worth all those tears, all the rage, all the demands not to shut out the thinking but hold onto it and trying to feel it (which I find absolutely bone-grindingly awful).

Of course, so practised am I at negative thinking that I immediately suggest that just as the good feelings had gone quickly when I was working with John, so too these feelings will go. I forget what Ruth said. It was something positive. But my mind was already off out the window, back on old familiar territory with all the old negative thoughts and feelings. However secure, warm and comforting those new feelings are, there is nothing quite like the old stuff we have lived with for years!

Then we both laughed because we both knew exactly what I was thinking!

If I let the old thoughts get back inside my brain, it is only because I let them. Well, that is what I think on a good day.

■ On reflection

It is now several months since I wrote those words above and now I am editing the book to get it ready to send off to my very patient editor. Those good feelings I described are in fact still with me – well, some of the time! They are not, though, always accompanied by tangible warm emotions as I have described them above. Sometimes I sit and meditate and feel quite ordinary, yet I am able to say to myself that I am OK. I'm getting beyond the lies I was told as a child.

I still have terrible 'down' times. I doubt my ability to write two articles I must get finished this week. I dread it that next week I have to go and talk to a group of teachers and spend an entire day leading their in-service training in their school. The day before doing that I will be overwhelmed with self-doubt and fear. I won't want to go. I will have to stop myself from saying, 'I can't do it.'

I have learnt that this terrible fear before a big event might well be there with me all through my life. Naively I used to think that after a few years of practice of leading days with teachers, the fear would go away! It doesn't. Sometimes I think I will give up that aspect of my teaching life because I go through such agonies. But as I learn to tell myself that I *can* do it, as I tell my inner trembling self that, even if I am sick with fear, I am still going to do it, I realize that there is a growing inner strength. Added to this I know that very gradually the fear is diminishing. I can now face a whole conference of people and I know I can do it – though the fear is pulsing the blood against my eardrums. And I always find at the end it was much better than I feared!

> **Going into the unknown is invariably frightening, but we learn what is significantly new only through adventures.**
>
> M. Scott Peck

■ An alternative to the negative

I know I can quite easily fill every day of the week with the negative junk! We can be so good at 'beating ourselves up' that we are almost addicted to it. St Paul had some good advice for how to get away from the negative stuff:

> **Fill your minds with everything that is true, everything that is noble, everything that is good and pure, everything that we love and honour, and everything that can be thought virtuous or worthy of praise.**
>
> St Paul, from Philippians 4:8

Although fear might hang around us and keep us in its icy clutches, and sometimes stifle those better feelings we have, we can still smile at those new and different feelings. We need to let ourselves feel the gladness that it really is possible to change our emotions, our thinking and our outlook on life, despite the various knocks we inevitably get just from living.

■ Thinking about good things

I have been working my way through a workbook for those who have been sexually abused (see the Resources section), and one of the activities was to ask someone to write a few things in the workbook about the good things they see in us. The suggestion was to ask your therapist or someone else you trust, so I asked Ruth to do it but suggested that she keep the workbook for a few days so that she could think about it.

She instantly replied that she didn't need to think about it and proceeded to write a list of the good things that she saw in me.

I was stunned.

I thought I needed to give her plenty of time as these things would be hard to find. But she just did it. In all the thinking about this book, that is the thing that has stuck in my mind.

So if you have someone whom you really trust and who loves and appreciates you, try asking them to tell you the good things that they see in you.

■ Beyond surviving

One of the things that I still struggle with is how much we can expect to leave our old life behind and start again. I find it alarming when people point to something in their life that they think will never change and will for ever trap them. Take the illness of depression, for example. Many people get better from depression and are never bothered by it again.

For me, I can see that for some reason, my depression keeps coming back (though nothing like as bad as it was 20 years ago), and I might need to accept that *maybe* it *might* bother me for the rest of my life.

But I absolutely refuse to call myself a 'depressive'! That has a ring of eternity about it! As if I am saying I am depressed now and will be now and for ever more. I *have* to believe that I can get beyond it.

It is like being a 'survivor' of sexual abuse, or cancer, or low self-esteem. How much do we let ourselves say and believe 'this has totally wrecked my life' with the implication that it will wreck our life for ever? Wouldn't we be much better to say, 'Yes, that did totally wreck my life – but I intend to get so far beyond it that I will one day be free of it and it will not influence my daily life at all?' That would be getting beyond thinking as a 'victim' and to start living as a real 'survivor'.

I don't have answers here. Just a sneaking suspicion that this could be another area where we are going to get what we expect to get.

■ Remember to laugh

Remember that if we laugh we feel better. If we learn to forgive and accept ourselves we laugh more and that spills over into the foundation of our being, our soul. Laughter of the soul is what Christians call joy – a deeply rooted sense that, despite uncertainties, all is well and we can smile at the world. When we laugh a lot we can see how joy can be linked with peace.

Positive Pointer

Laughing with someone can be communication at a very emotional deep level. It can give us a strong sense of belonging and of sharing.

1. Go back to the activity at the end of Chapter 3 where you started to think about writing a list of the things that you like about yourself. Try actually to write the list now, or add to it.

2. Ask someone to tell you what would be on their list about your good points.

3. Think about the people that put you down. Don't dwell on it. All that negative thinking isn't good for you. Just think about them long enough to realize that they probably put you down because they too lack self-esteem and the only way they can get to feel good is to tell themselves that they are better than you!

■ **Learn from this that putting others down is part of the negative behaviour that you want to get out of.**

■ **Consider the thought that they could be putting you down because they are actually envious of you! Now there's a thought. I am learning in therapy that envy pops up all over the place at the most unexpected times.**

33
Being Accepted

To live is to change, to live well is to change often.

Cardinal Newman

Many years ago now I went on a self-esteem day for women at my local adult education college. I was incredibly nervous about going but once I was there I found that everyone else was just as nervous as I was, so having to speak up and say who I was and why I had come was just about OK.

I was doing well during the day until we got near the end and we all had to stand in a circle and make positive statements about ourselves that we had previously practised in small groups. This was totally excruciating and I kept getting an irresistible urge to giggle, so I had to keep pretending I was blowing my nose.

One young woman had come to the group because she had left school with no qualifications and now wanted to go back to college. The leader for the day was making her stand up in the circle and assert that she was an intelligent woman and that she was going to succeed in her studies and so on.

The leader was a complete bully and the young woman clearly did not believe a word of it. She was intensely embarrassed, and close to tears.

■ 'What a load of rubbish!'

I said my positive bit about myself thinking that would stop the leader from bullying me, but the best moment came as we were nearly round the circle and one woman said the mantra she had practised then added, 'What a load of rubbish!' Everyone except the leader roared with laughter! For me it was the most real moment of the day.

The leader was then rather extraordinary. She told this woman off like a naughty schoolchild and she had to say her mantra over again – but this time everyone had silly grins on their faces.

Some of the books around about self-esteem do seem to me to go a bit over the top, a bit like that day at college. I am not at all sure we can just think ourselves into unlimited powers to become successful well-balanced people who find a superb partner and bring up wonderful children who all have good self-esteem and are successful – and all the rest of it. Saying over and over again to myself that I am a lovely human being or whatever it was I was saying that day, isn't in itself going to make me feel OK.

This is what Lewis Smedes says in his book *Shame and Grace* about this method of just reciting positive things:

> **[We can convince] ourselves that we are already acceptable enough. Usually we do this with self-congratulatory hype. Self-hypnosis is one method; we can recite self-esteem slogans, like mantras, every hour. However, it may be that if your brain tells your feelings that you are a terrific human being, your feelings may not be listening. Shame is usually too heavy to be ratcheted up by self-hypnosis.**

■ Positive thinking

I am sure Lewis Smedes is mostly right. However, rather unnervingly, I think the process we can go through to raise our self-esteem can include doing some things like that bossy leader was suggesting. Days like that can help us focus on the fact that we can change ourselves because it *does* work to set about replacing our negative thinking with positive thinking and getting ourselves into an 'I can do it' frame of mind.

We don't want just a mantra, though. That leaves out some important ingredients of change. We want time and thought to go into ourselves gradually developing real change within. My feelings of fear of being alone and abandoned in this strange world are not going to go away just because I do some kind of positive brainwashing. But in the long run (not just one day), telling ourselves positive things can help us begin to change those negative 'old tapes'. But the damage is much deeper than that. As one person put it to me as I researched for this book:

I feel totally unacceptable to God. I'm sure he wants nothing to do with me.

Brian, age 45

Betrayed trust in childhood and our fear of abandonment and so on, is so deeply influential, it is unrealistic to think that is going to disappear like dew on a spider's web when the sun comes up. Our betrayed trust is so deep that it connects with the spiritual bit of ourselves that is longing for some kind of mystical comfort – our God-shaped hole.

■ I am accepted

My bottom-line in all this change from who I was to what I want to be is that I feel accepted by God. This is the other essential ingredient.

Yes, I am accepted and loved by my wonderful family and that is fantastic. Therapy is a time to feel accepted by some stranger who becomes a trusted guide, friend and 'mother'.

But for me this is not enough. It still does not totally satisfy me that I am accepted.

For me that ultimate knowledge that I am an OK person is only that I know in my inner life, my soul, I have crept into the huge hand of God and I nestle there, warm, comforted, safe and above all, accepted as a child of God. I have come home.

Whatever happens, however many bulldozers there are, and however much I might be, or feel, abandoned, abused or rejected by those around me, I know that I am held. Safe. Accepted for who I am and loved more than I could ever imagine.

This is what Christians call 'grace'.

In grace something is overcome; grace occurs 'in spite of' something; grace occurs in spite of estrangement and separation. Grace is the reunion of life with life, the reconciliation of the self with itself. Grace is the acceptance of that which is rejected. Grace transforms fate into a meaningful destiny; it changes guilt into confidence and courage. There is something triumphant in the word 'grace'; in spite of the abounding of sin grace abounds much more...

Sometimes... a wave of light breaks into our darkness, and it is as though a voice were saying: 'You are accepted. *You are accepted*, accepted by that which is greater than you, and the name of which you do not know. Do not ask for the name now; perhaps you will find it later. Do not try to do anything now; perhaps later you will do much. Do not seek for anything; do not perform anything; do not intend anything. *Simply accept the fact that you are accepted!*'

Paul Tillich, *The Shaking of the Foundations*

Positive Pointer

You are accepted!

Activity

1. Look out for self-esteem days at colleges and those run by mental health charities.

2. You are your own worst enemy if you keep blaming and criticizing yourself. You must stop blaming and pointing out the bad things! Work on letting yourself feel accepted.

Saying to yourself 'I forgive you' is tough, but you must do it if you are to move on to that brighter future where you develop who you really are and start to smile at the world.

If you are like me you, and try to do something tough, you do it, but then completely forget to stop and feel good about it. I am brilliant at letting a success just pass by and then start working towards the next goal! We need all the positive reinforcement we can get, so start practising. Learn to stop and say, 'Well done'!

34
Making an Action Plan

You cannot discover new oceans unless you have the courage to lose sight of the shore.

A poster on a wall in a college in India

If we really want to achieve those things that we call our hopes, dreams and ambitions, we need to have an action plan and there is one suggestion for how to do this as the activity for this chapter.

We need an action plan because it is a dominant feature in those who don't feel OK about themselves that we tend to put things off, partly presumably because we don't believe we can achieve what we want to do, but partly also because of ordinary human apathy.

It is, after all, very much easier to be a couch potato than it is to be the leading light in our community on the subject of guinea-pig handling, or the person everyone consults when they want to take a group of 10 small children on a birthday outing to the zoo.

Apathy, inertia and a belief that we just cannot do it can stop us realizing our dreams every bit as much as if we lose the use of our limbs, or our sight, or something else happens to change our lives dramatically.

■ Heading for adventure

Adventure is the meeting of dreams and reality.

I have this quote on a poster on my study wall. I look at it often to remind myself that life is an adventure, and to remember that we can turn our dreams into real happenings.

I believe that it is when we set out to realize our dreams that we are being true to ourselves and allowing ourselves to become more truly human.

■ Who will we ask to help us?

For most of us, working through a self-help book like this can help us to focus on what we really want to do. But at some stage, we can get much further towards achieving our ambitions if we also have someone who will listen and encourage us. If you feel you don't have enough support, think through how you could get some more.

The kind of people to ask are those who:

- **are good listeners.**
- **are sensitive and caring.**
- **love us.**
- **are non-judgmental.**
- **don't dump all their 'stuff' on you when you are only just able to manage your own 'stuff'!**
- **are good friends and we enjoy being with them.**

Someone with just one of these characteristics would be great. With two or more, you are on to a good thing. Share some of this book with them and tell them what you are trying to do. Outline your action plan for the next week, and the next year, and ask them to help you by talking through your progress from time to time.

If you can afford counselling or therapy, visit a few counsellors for a preliminary session before you select which person is the best one for you and your needs.

■ Action plans can be very powerful

What an action plan can do for us is change our vague ideas that we might like to feel better about ourselves into actually taking the first step. To set out on our aim of learning to feel better about ourselves can be such a huge task, that unless we break it down into manageable bits, we are likely to feel overwhelmed and give up.

It is like making a list of things to do today when you are finding life tough. You *must* start your list with very small, easy things. Someone suggested to me yesterday that our list can start with 'Inhale, exhale, inhale, exhale'! Wonderful advice!

Make it *your* action plan by adapting my ideas to fit what you need. If you believe it to be *your* action plan, you will find that hugely empowering. It isn't me, Sue, who is getting you going on improving the quality of your life, it is *you*.

■ What is my motive?

Working with teachers in their professional development as both teachers and human beings, I have found that if we ask ourselves *why* we want to achieve our particular dreams and ambitions, in some way it seems to give us the motivation to see our plans through, and act on them to make real change in our life.

Perhaps your aim is to become more confident in public. If you keep reminding yourself why you want this, it gives the whole thing much more power and meaning. So you might say something like this:

'I want to be more confident in public so that I will come over better at an interview, then I would go for a better job and this will change my life for the better.'

If your small step to attain that larger ambition was to join a self-help group and find like-minded people to talk to, then that would be the first part of your action plan. It narrows down the big things into something smaller you can do this week.

Positive Pointer

If we are clear why we want to achieve things, we will have more drive to do them.

Activity

Getting ready to write an action plan
Here are some preliminary lists to work on before you start on the main action plan.

These are the things that I want to achieve in my life:

■ **writing a short story and sending it in for a competition**

■ **climbing up every mountain in Britain**

■ **visiting every bird reserve in Britain**

and so on.
This is why I want to do these things:

■ **I have always wanted to do that since I was a child.**

■ **I really enjoy ......, it makes me feel good, and so on.**

My action plan
This activity can be spread over several weeks and it is one to come back to again and again. The list you make needs to be referred to often, so put the paper where you can see it. Get a whole sheet of paper and divide it into three sections:

■ **In the first section, write fairly easy things you can do this week (e.g. stop watching the television news because it is confrontational and depressing and listen to five minutes of radio news instead and use the extra time you have gained to do something creative).**

■ **In the second section write things that are a bit harder and that might need more time to achieve (e.g. go to the library and borrow some tapes to learn enough of a new language just to get by on a**

weekend trip abroad; or actually start a journal to see if writing
helps you to make your thinking and feeling clearer to you).

■ In the third section list things that are longer term or things
that you might need help with (e.g. join a self-help group (see the
Resources list); or make a determined effort in your journal to turn
around your negative thinking over the next few months).

Do not wait. Start your action plan now. Those with low self-
esteem can be some of the world's more gifted procrastinators.

35
Becoming Real

It is through love that we elevate ourselves. And it is through our love for others that we assist others to elevate themselves.

M. Scott Peck

I have agonized for ages about how I was going to write the last chapter of this book. I have had many tries at it, but each time it isn't right, and I feel such a hypocrite. My negative self-talk takes over and I end up dropping tears into the keyboard of my word processor.

But today I know exactly how to finish the book. I am sitting on the sofa with my little dog Annie beside me. She is just over a year old and despite the great efforts of the vet, she is going to die. Her kidneys have stopped working and several tries at getting them going again have given only temporary relief.

We have her back from the vet for the weekend so that we can say goodbye to her. All the family are here and we are taking lots of photos. Annie is comfortable enough, the vet says, for a couple of days.

I am meant to be the other side of the country today giving a talk in Cardiff to carers of depressed people. I wanted to go so much. I hate letting people down and I so much want to help hurting people as being able to share something of my struggle is about the only way I can make sense of all that past pain. The whole idea that the wounded can help to heal others is something that keeps me sane. But I knew I couldn't go to do my talk today, despite the guilt trip which I inevitably went on for a few hours. I have to be at home with my children and my little dog.

■ Living to love

I went to fetch my laptop computer so that I could sit here and write. I am going to spend the whole day beside Annie. She likes me to be here and I like touching her and reassuring her.

In one of those rare moments of emotional clarity I found I suddenly know why I find it so hard to manage life. There is one crucial thing that I know I *can* do, and that is to love.

The more I think about this as my little dog's life slips away from her I can see that, though I find it difficult to believe myself to be a 'together' person, or a person who has much value, I do clamber out from behind my brick wall in order to share my love.

When I think of people I admire or love, they too share their love, even if they are very wounded people who need to retreat to their own safe place. Not to love is to remove ourselves from the very heart of what it is to be alive. Not to love is to stay behind our brick wall for ever and to put so little into relationships, into life, into being truly human, that we stagnate and real life ebbs out of us.

■ Love hurts

We cannot protect ourselves in some magical way from pain however hard we try. We can do our best to keep pain away by trying to keep all our relationships superficial. (Lots of people seem to do this with great success!)

It just is hurtful to love. The person may die, reject us, hurt us, stop loving us completely and abandon us. But to follow our dreams and get the most out of our short life, it seems to me that we must risk that hurt because people (and animals) are so precious that they are worth the hurt. They are worth us making ourselves vulnerable out there in the world beyond the safety of the wall.

I fully acknowledged 11 months ago, when I chose Annie from all the other puppies, that if I love her, one day I would be hurt. (For some reason our Great Creator designed dogs to live so much shorter than humans that I am sure it must be forgivable for me to think that this was a cruel bit of organization of the universe. Though as my daughter points out, at least as we survive each doggy death, it prepares us for the death of humans we love.)

■ Unconditional love

I think in my better moments, between my tears, that Annie was worth all the pain I feel and the pain I see on my children's faces. She wouldn't have been half the fun if we had held back and limited the amount of love we gave her. It was unconditional love from the start – and she knew that.

It is exactly that kind of unconditional love that we need to give to ourselves. I am not good at doing that for myself, but today as I sit here, I realize I have learnt more about unconditional love.

We can all love, or learn to love. Even if we feel we have never been deeply loved, people are able to turn that around and become loving and feel love for themselves. It is not easy. I think I would say it was true of me that no one had ever deeply loved me (though maybe my grandparents did but I had limited contact with them) until I met my partner while I was at college. I know others who haven't had much love, but they are able to reach out and love others, so I know a life with little love can give and receive love.

■ Becoming real

I believe that it is as we give ourselves to others out there beyond the wall that we become true human beings - 'real' people. We are *really* living. Despite all our self-hatred and despair of ourselves as hopeless, we can bring love, joy and peace to others.

'What is REAL?' asked the Rabbit one day, when they were lying side by side near the nursery fender,

before Nana came to tidy the room. 'Does it mean having things that buzz inside you and a stick-out handle?'

'Real isn't how you are made', said the Skin Horse. 'It's a thing that happens to you. When a child really loves you for a long time, not just to play with, but REALLY loves you, then you become Real.'

'Does it hurt?' asked the Rabbit.

'Sometimes,' said the Skin Horse, for he was always truthful. 'When you are Real you don't mind being hurt.'

'Does it happen all at once, like being wound up,' he asked, 'or bit by bit?'

'It doesn't happen all at once', said the Skin Horse. 'You become. It takes a long time... Generally, by the time you are Real, most of your hair has been loved off, and your eyes drop out... But these things don't matter at all, because once you are Real you can't be ugly except to people who don't understand... Once you are Real you can't become unreal again. It lasts for always.'

Margery Williams, *The Velveteen Rabbit*

■ Risking all

But the real crunch is that as soon as we set out to love, we are risking being hurt. We have to take the risk. In fact I think we have to risk *everything* to love. That must be why I see such devastation in the eyes of friends when a partner walks out on them after years of loving and living. To love is to believe that in all the pain and chaos of our world, at least that love is secure. Certain. Timeless. For ever.

As I sit here I am grappling with the thought that maybe it is because we love that we find life so difficult to manage. The hurt is so great when something goes wrong. Were we to refuse to love, life would presumably be free of the pain I feel today. But would it be a life worth living to refuse to love?

■ Refusing to give ourselves to others

We all probably know people who will not risk loving. I found quite a few of them as I researched this book. They seemed to me to be among the saddest people I have ever met. I cried over some of their stories and I wanted so much to be able to help them.

Some of them whom I talked to face to face knew exactly what they were doing. They would openly say that they had no intention whatsoever of risking anything. They had been hurt before and were not going to let it happen again.

But some of them hoped anyway for a partner. For a family. For love. For security. For a home. For a career.

The puzzle is, will they ever attain that if they will not risk? I suspect not just yet. They need time and a great deal of help, love, and maybe a good therapist in order to change from their defensive position in their risk-free environment behind their wall. I felt enormous guilt that I couldn't help them. I didn't know how to.

The good news, and the end of this book, is that people can and do change. Some change can be quite fast. I have changed today sitting here beside Annie. I am thinking positive things about myself. I love. I risk. I will somehow be able to pick myself up from Annie's death, though at the moment that seems impossible. The sense of devastation is so powerful.

■ Getting it together

Some change is much slower and takes years of trying, failing, and trying again before we get ourselves together. There is no easy route, but I have found that the results are wonderful!

We will always need great courage to be risk-takers, but if you have read this book, you obviously are a risk-taker. (Stop all that negative self-talk that tells you you are not!)

Nothing about risking, or loving, or changing how we think or what we do, is easy. These things that make up the essence of life will always be demanding. Life is just like that.

I have a picture in my study that I look at every day. It is a penguin completely stuck in a crevasse and the words on the picture are:

If this is the first day of the rest of my life... I'm in a lot of trouble.

I love that saying! It is sufficiently negative to appeal to my gloomy Eeyorish view of life, but is also very funny and very realistic about our human situation as we try to make sense of the paradoxes we face each day and try to manage life.

■ The bottom line

Pulling all this together, I think that throughout the book there are four main aspects to the many strategies I have proposed to help us out from behind our brick wall:

1. If we have suffered in the past and are left with low self-esteem, we will find that we have an inner strength because of the suffering that those who didn't suffer in that way don't have. (I am definitely not saying that what happened to us was 'good'! I am saying that it can be empowering to share our inner strength with others and that being a 'wounded healer' is one way to make sense of our suffering.)
2. We need to develop a really good relationship with ourselves, loving and caring for our 'inner child', looking after our body, taking time to meditate, setting out to make our dreams and ambitions a reality, and so on.
3. We need to spread love, joy and peace to others and by this giving of ourselves, in some remarkable way, we find ourselves.
4. If you can, try to think of yourself as already accepted by the Great Creator. You *are* accepted and your unique value is acknowledged.

■ Everyone is special

So I wish you well with your rainbow book. Go back through it with a different colour pen and try to do some of the activities that seemed impossible last time.

Remember that you are special. Everyone is. There are no exceptions. Tell yourself every day that you are special and that you are going to follow your hopes and dreams and get the most out of life.

And whatever you do, don't forget to laugh and have times of being utterly silly!

May the road rise up to meet you,
May the wind be always at your back,
May the sun shine warm on your face, the rain fall
  softly on your fields;
  and until we meet again,
May God hold you in the palm of his hand.

Based on a Celtic blessing

Resources

■ Useful addresses

For self-help groups
Depression Alliance, 35 Westminster Bridge Road, London, SE1 7JB, tel: 020 7633 0557

MIND: ring 020 8519 2122 to find out about your local branch of MIND and groups in your area.

General advice and resources for self-esteem
Titus Alexander at The Self-Esteem Network, 32 Carisbrooke Road, London, E17 7EF, tel: 020 8521 6977. They publish *The Self-Esteem Directory*, edited by Titus Alexander, a great resource for ideas, books and tapes, etc.

For those struggling with results of sexual abuse
Ellen Bass and Laura Davis, *The Courage to Heal*, Cedar.
Laura Davis, *The Courage to Heal Workbook*, Harper and Row.

For a range of mail-order resources on self-esteem and other mental-health issues (many for teachers and parents) contact: Smallwood Publishing, The Old Bakery, Charlton House, Dour Street, Dover, Kent, CT16 1ED, tel: 01304 226800. They are on-line at www.smallwood.co.uk.

For meditating
David Adam, *The Edge of Glory*, Triangle/SPCK.
Meryl Doney, *The Art of Prayer*, Lion Publishing.
M. Scott Peck, *Meditations on the Road*, Simon and Schuster.
Andy Raine, et al., *Celtic Daily Prayer*, Marshall Pickering/HarperCollins.
Veronica Zundel, *Famous Prayers*, Lion Publishing.
Robert Van de Weyer, *Celtic Prayers*, Hunt and Thorpe.

■ Further reading

Sue Atkinson, *Climbing Out of Depression*, Lion Publishing.
Dr Roger Baker, *Understanding Panic Attacks and Overcoming Fear*, Lion Publishing.
Lucia Capaccione, *Recovery of Your Inner Child*, Simon and Schuster.
Robert Holden, *Laughter: The Best Medicine*, Thorsons.
Susan Jeffers, *Feel the Fear and Do It Anyway*, Arrow Books.
Gael Lindenfield, *Self-Esteem*, Thorsons.
Gael Lindenfield, *Super Confidence*, Thorsons.
Dorothy Rowe, *The Successful Self*, Fontana.
Dorothy Rowe, *Wanting Everything*, Fontana.
Lewis Smedes, *Forgive and Forget*, Harper and Row.
Lewis Smedes, *Shame and Grace*, Triangle/SPCK.
Claire Walmsley, *Assertiveness*, BBC Books.
Charles L. Whitfield, *Boundaries and Relationships*, Health Communications, Inc.

For teachers, and other individuals and professionals in education, health, family life, work and crime prevention etc. contact Smallwood Publishing (see address above) and ask for *The Self-Esteem Directory*.

Jenny Mosely, *Quality Circle Time in the Primary Classroom*, LDA.

Tony Humphreys, *Self-Esteem: The Key to Your Child's Education*, Newleaf.

■ For teenage girls

Anita Naik, *Self-Esteem*, Hodder Headline.

■ For more details about personality types

David Keirsey and Marilyn Bates, *Please Understand Me: Character and Temperament Types*, Prometheus Nemesis Books.

■ For personality types and their relationship to learning

Gordon Lawrence, *People Types and Tiger Stripes*, Centre for Applications of Psychological Type, Inc.

Other books published by Lion:

CLIMBING OUT OF DEPRESSION
A Practical Guide for Sufferers

Sue Atkinson

'This is wise stuff, with resonance that lingers on long after it is over, none more than the hope it offers, born of experience.'

Anne Pilling, *The Door*

Being depressed often leaves you feeling paralysed into inaction. Climbing back out of the pit of gloom seems almost impossible. You need help, and that is what this book offers – practical, humane and spiritual help.

Sue Atkinson has suffered years of depression herself. She does not write as an expert on depression, or as a depression counsellor, but as someone who knows the feelings from close personal experience. As a result her book contains a varied menu of hints, quotations and illustrations, not page after page of unbroken text.

This is a book to dip into as fits your mood and the need of the moment, making a dependable guide to the climb.

ISBN 0 7459 2248 1 (paperback)

UNDERSTANDING PANIC ATTACKS AND OVERCOMING FEAR

Dr Roger Baker

What is a panic attack?

What does it feel like?

What causes attacks?

Can they be cured?

This highly authoritative yet practical book helps the reader towards an in-depth understanding of panic. In clear and concise language it describes a psychological self-help programme for panic sufferers.

'A full recovery is possible,' explains Dr Baker. 'It certainly is not easy, nor quick, but it definitely is possible.'

ISBN 0 7459 3313 0 (paperback)

All Lion books are available from your local bookshop, or can be ordered via our website or from Marston Book Services. For a free catalogue, showing the complete list of titles available, please contact:

Customer Services
Marston Book Services
PO Box 269
Abingdon
Oxon
OX14 4YN

Tel: 01235 465500
Fax: 01235 465555

Our website can be found at:
www.lion-publishing.co.uk

SHREWSBURY COLLEGE
RADBROOK LRC